EUDORA WELTY

MODERN LITERATURE SERIES

GENERAL EDITOR: Philip Winsor

In the same series:

    (continued on last page of book)

EUDORA WELTY

Elizabeth Evans

7458

FREDERICK UNGAR PUBLISHING CO.
NEW YORK

Copyright © 1981 by Frederick Ungar Publishing Co., Inc.
Printed in the United States of America
Design by Anita Duncan

Library of Congress Cataloging in Publication Data

Evans, Elizabeth, 1935–
  Eudora Welty.

  (Modern literature series)
  Bibliography: p.
  Includes index.
  1. Welty, Eudora, 1909–   —Criticism and interpretation.
I. Title.   II. Series: Modern literature series.
PS3545.E6Z68   813'.52   81-2812
ISBN 0-8044-2187-0   AACR2

The letters by John Rood and John Woodburn appearing in Chapter 1 are used by courtesy of Mrs. John Rood and Mr. Charles Woodburn respectively.

The excerpts from *What Year Is This?* by Eudora Welty and Hildegard Dolson are used by courtesy of Russell & Volkening.

For C. Hugh Holman

Contents

Chronology

1909   On April 13, Eudora Alice Welty is born in Jackson, Mississippi, to Mary Chestina and Christian Webb Welty.

1925   Graduates from Central High School, Jackson.

1925–27   Attends Mississippi State College for Women, Columbus.

1927–29   Earns B.A. degree, University of Wisconsin, Madison.

1930–31   Studies advertising at Columbia University School of Business, New York City.

1931   Christian Webb Welty dies; Eudora Welty returns to Jackson to live.

1931–33   Works for various newspapers and for Jackson radio station WJDX.

1933–36   Works as publicity agent for WPA in Mississippi and begins taking photographs of people encountered in her work.

1936   WPA job ends. Has a one-man show of photographs in Photographic Galleries, New York City. Publishes first stories: "Death of a Traveling Salesman" and "Magic."

1940   Diarmuid Russell, son of the Irish poet George Russell, becomes her literary agent. Attends summer conference at Breadloaf.

1941   "A Worn Path" wins second prize, O. Henry Memorial Contest Award. Has summer at Yaddo.

Publishes *A Curtain of Green*, with an introduction by Katherine Anne Porter.

1942   Publishes *The Robber Bridegroom*; "The Wide Net" wins first prize in O. Henry Memorial Contest Award.

1942–43   Receives Guggenheim Fellowship.

1943   Follows her editor John Woodburn to Harcourt Brace and publishes *The Wide Net and Other Stories*. "Livvie Is Back" wins first prize, O. Henry Memorial Contest Award.

1944   Receives $1,000 award from American Academy of Arts and Letters. Serves on *New York Times Book Review* staff for six months. Uses pseudonym of Michael Ravenna for reviews of World War II battle reports from North Africa, Europe, and South Pacific.

1946   Publishes *Delta Wedding*.

1947   Lectures at Pacific Northwest Writers' Conference; stays three months in San Francisco.

1948   Publishes *Music from Spain* (story).

1949   Publishes *The Golden Apples*.

1949–50   Receives renewal of Guggenheim Fellowship allowing travel to France, Italy, and England.

1950   Publishes *Short Stories* (essay).

1951   "The Burning" wins second prize, O. Henry Memorial Contest Award.

1952   Elected to National Institute of Arts and Letters; travels in Europe, England, and Ireland.

1954   Publishes *The Ponder Heart* and *Selected Stories*.

1955   Travels to Europe; participates in conference on American studies at Cambridge University and delivers lecture, "Place in Fiction." Publishes *The Bride of Innisfallen*. Receives the William Dean Howells Medal of the Academy of Arts and Letters for *The Ponder Heart*.

1956   Dramatization of *The Ponder Heart* opens on Broadway.

1957   Publishes *Place in Fiction* (essay).

1958   Honorary Consultant in American Letters, Library of Congress.

1958–59 Receives Lucy Donnelley Fellowship Award from Bryn Mawr College.

1960   Receives Ingram Memorial Foundation Award in Literature.

1962   Publishes *Three Papers on Fiction*.

1964   Publishes *The Shoe Bird* (Juvenile).

1965   Publishes *Thirteen Stories*, with an introduction by Ruth M. Vande Kieft (reprint of previously published stories).

1969   Publishes *A Sweet Devouring* (autobiographical essay).

1970   Receives Edward McDowell Medal. Publishes *Losing Battles*.

1971   Publishes *One Time, One Place: Mississippi in the Depression, A Snapshot Album*, with an introduction by Eudora Welty. Becomes member of American Academy of Arts and Letters.

1972   Publishes *The Optimist's Daughter*. Receives the Gold Medal for Fiction.

1973   Receives the Pulitzer Prize for *The Optimist's Daughter*.

1974   Publishes *A Pageant of Birds* (essay).

1975   Publishes *Fairy Tale of the Natchez Trace* (lecture).

1978   Publishes *The Eye of the Story. Selected Essays and Reviews*.

1979   Publishes *Ida M'Toy* (essay).

1980   Receives the National Medal of Literature for past and continuing contributions to literature, and the Medal of Freedom Award.

        Publishes *The Collected Stories of Eudora Welty*.

1981   Publishes "Bye-Bye Brevoort" (revue sketch).

1

∿·∿·∿·∿·∿·∿·∿·∿·∿·∿·∿·∿·∿·∿·

Woman of Letters:
Great Descents
of Good Fortune

The literary career of Eudora Welty now spans forty-five years, her stories and novels occupy a significant place in American fiction, and she herself is without question one of the two or three most important women writers the South has produced. With her first publication, discerning readers knew that hers was an extraordinary talent, finding in her work fresh insights into the human condition presented in a style marked by clarity, sureness of image and dialogue, and richness in humor and technical skill. Both the South and the nation have honored her, the year 1980 alone bringing her the National Medal for Literature and the Medal of Freedom as well as a state dinner hosted by Mississippi's governor and his wife. Other awards, grants, and honorary degrees have been received, she has been interviewed by scholars and journalists, and symposia are conducted on her work; yet she has remained modest and unassuming, living always at home in Jackson, Mississippi.

Interviews and articles provide some information about Eudora Welty's life, but she turns a shy and discouraging look toward the biographer, declaring that a writer's work should be everything. Persuaded to deposit her manuscripts in the Department of Archives and History in Jackson,[1] Miss Welty kept back "a trunk full of stuff" which she considered nobody else's concern. The prospects to the biographer are slim at the moment;

to the hopeful editor of letters, they are slight indeed. "Your private life should be kept private," she has said. "My own, I don't think would particularly interest anybody, for that matter. But I'd guard it; I feel strongly about that. They'd have a hard time trying to find something about me. I think I'd better burn everything up. It's best to burn letters, but at least I've never kept diaries or journals."[2]

Eudora Alice Welty was born on April 13, 1909, in Jackson, Mississippi. Her father, Christian Webb Welty, was from Ohio and her mother, Chestina Andrews, from West Virginia. Miss Welty and her two brothers grew up in a household of readers, where the encyclopedia was kept in the dining room to settle dinnertable questions and where books included the ancient poets, Dante, Shakespeare, Milton, English and French novelists, folk and fairy tales, as well as contemporary writers like Yeats and Virginia Woolf. Childhood activities were the sort ideally associated with the pre-industrialized South. Davis Elementary School was across the street from the Welty front yard. Also within walking distance were the ice cream parlor, the grocery store, the two movie houses, and Smith Park where whole families drifted after supper to listen to the band play selections from William Tell and other favorites. At the nearby state capitol, children rode their bicycles down terraces and stairs, skated over the marble floors, and flew kites on the lawn. Other pleasures included the Pythian Castle swimming pool and a summer camp that provided background for the story "Moon Lake."[3] Trips to the public library (recounted in "A Sweet Devouring") were subject to Miss Annie Parker's rules of tiptoeing in silence and borrowing only two books. The latter rule, Miss Welty has quipped, held "until you were dead. You could be eighty-five years old and could still just take out two books. I always wanted more."[4] Piano lessons were under Amanda Stewart Buck's direction, and music has proved a rich

allusive source in Miss Welty's fiction. A memorable
event in those early years was the Sunday visits to her
father's office in the Lamar Life Insurance Company, a
firm named after a prominent Mississippian who bore
the Faulknerian name Lucius Quintus Cincinnatus
Lamar. Although Miss Welty says her father's office was
probably typical of the time, on those visits it was "a
fascinating if airless Paradise." All three Welty children
tried out the dictaphone (the first one in Jackson), which
"gave back a ghostly version of my father's own voice,
speaking riddles meant for the ears of Miss Josephine
Wright."[5] While her brothers swung on the mahogany
gate in front of the safe, Miss Welty, somewhat propheti-
cally, fell in love with the typewriter and "all those
polished keys which, if only hit right or long enough,
might write anything at all."

From 1925 to 1927, Miss Welty attended Mississippi
State College for Women. She received a B.A. in 1929
from the University of Wisconsin and spent the years
1930–1931 in New York studying advertising at Columbia University. The Depression made advertising jobs
scarce so she returned to Jackson in 1931, the same year
her father died at fifty-two. One of Christian Welty's last
projects was the establishing of the radio station WJDX,
which was housed in the top of the Lamar Life Building.
The station gave Miss Welty her first job, the kind a
young girl considered ideal, she remarked years later—
part time and vague. Some of its aspects, however, were
specific, such as securing talent to fill in when WJDX did
not get programming from NBC, editing a little newsletter, and printing the weekly program schedule for listeners. The small staff wrote and mailed its own fan letters,
at least one of which praised the scheduling of the Metro-
politan Opera radio broadcasts.[6]

What Miss Welty has described as various meager
jobs on newspapers followed. In 1933, she became a
publicity agent for the newly founded WPA (Works

Progress Authority), a job which ended with the 1936 election. Before her work with WPA, for Miss Welty Mississippi had meant Jackson, Columbus, and an occasional visit to the coast; afterward she had seen the state interviewing people, setting up booths at fairs, and taking photographs on her own. The experience "was the real germ of my wanting to become a real writer, a true writer. It caused me to seriously attempt it. It made me see, for the first time, what life was really like in this state. It was a revelation."[7] As we shall see in detail later, "real" writing had been steadily and privately going on, and when the WPA job ended, Miss Welty's first published story, "Death of a Traveling Salesman," appeared in *Manuscript*, a little magazine published in Athens, Ohio.

Brief biographical notes in reviews of Miss Welty's early work reveal that she listened to a great deal of music (especially Mozart); that she liked picnicking, raising camellias, traveling low speed, astronomy, and Bea Lillie records; and that she avoided big parties and preferred small gatherings of close friends. Admirers and acquaintances can add other information about the writer and the person, but little surpasses Elizabeth Bowen's account of Miss Welty's visit to Ireland and her stay at Bowen's Court, an occasion she described in a letter to Charles Ritchie.

You know my passion for her works. She had apparently drifted over to Dublin on her own. She sent me a telegram from there and I asked her to come down and stay. . . . I take to her immensely and I think you would. She's very un-writerish and *bien élevée*. A Southern girl from the State of Mississippi; quiet, self-contained, easy, outwardly old-fashioned, very funny indeed when she starts talking. . . . She's reserved (in itself, I think, a good point these days) so although we have chatted away a good deal, I really know little about her life, nor she about mine. I think she's like me in preferring places to people, and any unexpected sight or view while we are driving about

the country makes her start up in the car with a smothered cry
as though she had been stung by a wasp. . . . No one would
pick her out on sight as "an interesting woman." Actually I
think she's a genius rather than an interesting woman, which I
am glad of as I prefer the former.[8]

In the spring of 1951, Miss Welty again stayed
at Bowen's Court, and Elizabeth Bowen reported to
Blanche Knopf that "Eudora Welty is staying in the
house—working away at one of her great short stories
in another room. This is ideal: I'm so fond of her, and
her preoccupation during the day with her own work
gives me a freedom unknown when one has an ordinary 'social' guest."

   Eudora Welty has never aligned herself with any
writers' group, and as an artist at work has remained a
solitary figure, loving to see writers "when they coincide
with my friends, but not just *as* writers. You work by
yourself."[9] Nor has she felt deprived as a writer because
she is a woman: "All that talk of women's lib doesn't
apply *at all* to women writers. We've always been able to
do what we've wished."[10] She has set a high standard of
integrity and perseverance in her work and disagrees
with those who claim we never really become ourselves
until we are dead. Her own view reflects an essential
difference: "It is by living on, it seems to me now, that
the way of real honesty lies. The realest possible honesty
is come by, attained, earned if you like, by continuing."

   In a June 1942 interview, Miss Welty described her
earliest work to Robert Van Gelder, establishing then
the cornerstone of place. Those early stories "were awful," she said.

I'm from Jackson, Mississippi, and never had been much of
anywhere else, but the action in my stories took place in Paris.
They were awful. I remember the first line in one of them:
"Monsieur Boule deposited a delicate dagger in Mademoiselle's
left side and departed with a poised immediacy." This, of
course, makes no sense at all. I loved the "poised immediacy" so

much that I've remembered the whole sentence. . . . Then I went home and started writing about what I knew. I was older and I guess had a little more sense, enough sense so that I could see the great rift between what I wrote and what was the real thing.[11]

Miss Welty's return to Jackson in 1931 marked the beginning of her writing seriously "in a solitary intuitive way, in an attempt to capture the mysterious atmosphere of places and the elusive, revealing actions and gestures of the people she encountered."[12] Her earliest stories showed "all the weaknesses of the headlong. I never rewrote, I just wrote. The plots in these stories are weak because I didn't know enough to worry about plots."[13]

A question mark accompanies the dates on some manuscripts from 1930 to 1937, notably "A Ghost Story" (1930?), "Acrobats in a Park" (1934?), "The Children" (1934?), "The Waiting Room" (1935), "Beautiful Ohio" (1936?), "The Doll" (1936?), "Magic" (1936), and "Retreat" (1937). Of the group, only four have been published.[14] Another work of this time, "Death of a Traveling Salesman" (1936) was, unlike the others, included in her later collections. These stories vary in subject matter, style, and theme, but their existence is of great importance, especially to the student, who finds tantalizing clues here to Welty's later work.

"The Waiting Room," described as a farce for little theater, is set in the railroad station of a small southern town, a setting Miss Welty would use in a later and far more serious story, "The Key" (1941). "The Waiting Room" brings together a miniature ship of fools. Central among the would-be passengers is Violet, who is running away from her husband Emil. Her nervousness prompts her lover Thomas to mutter, "Shut up, dear. Do you want the whole world to know we're running away?" a line that later appears (with slight change) as the title "The Whole World Knows," Eugene MacLain's story in *The Golden Apples*. There is also a funny old lady who recognizes and talks to Danny Boy (the Detroit Demobilizer, a wrestler with a dizzy wife and a jealous mistress), Myron (who holds a snake in a box), a Camera Man, Gresham and Art (railroad men), and, finally, Violet's husband Emil. The plot is less memorable perhaps than a brief exchange between the two railroad men where a line of dialogue appears that later found its way into one of Miss Welty's most frequently anthologized stories. Gresham lectures, "Accommodate the passengers, Roy, is the motto of the F. and L. G. Railroad," and Art retorts, "Aw, if you're so smart, why ain't you rich," the words Billy Boy hurls at Leota to end "Petrified Man."

"A Ghost Story" and "The Doll" suggest the elusive and mysterious inner experiences that Welty characters undergo, while "Magic" contains the precise details that characterize her work. Its heroine, Myrtle Cross, who wears a rose-colored crepe-de-chine dress and Sheer-O-Sheer stockings, has bought by mail from Kansas City a small, lusterless "Magic Love Philtre" for ten cents plus a coupon clipped from a movie magazine. As Jan Nordby Gretlund has pointed out, Tina in "Acrobats in the Park" introduces the outsider, one who invades a family by marrying into it and thus threatens its original unity. This theme recurs in later works: in *Delta Wedding*, when Robbie Reid threatens the Fairchild clan by marrying George, in *Losing Battles*, when Gloria marries Jack Renfro, and in *The Optimist's Daughter*, when Wanda Fay Chisom marries Judge Clinton McKelva.

Miss Welty showed these early works to no one, but did ask her Jackson neighbor and friend Hubert Creekmore for names and addresses of people to whom she might send some of her stories. It was Creekmore who suggested John Rood, the editor of *Manuscript*. When Rood accepted "Death of a Traveling Salesman" and "Magic" for publication, Creekmore and Miss Welty were both flabbergasted, but her writing career had officially begun. The extant correspondence from John

Rood to Eudora Welty (in the Eudora Welty Collection at the Department of Archives and History, Jackson) sheds some light on the magazine itself and on the enthusiasm its editors expressed over their discovery.

Manuscript, a bimonthly magazine published in Athens, Ohio, was edited by Mary Lawhead and John Rood, husband and wife. Miss Welty has described these editors as rare. In 1936, the last year *Manuscript* was published, Rood described it as being nearly three years old and, "like most literary magazines, 'in the red' all the time!" Nevertheless, Rood claimed to have found and encouraged "a dozen or so really gifted young writers." *Manuscript* authors received no pay; indeed, if the Roods had not owned their own printery (Lawhead Press), the expense of producing *Manuscript* would have been prohibitive. Financial worries were in part compensated for by the attention *Manuscript* received. John Rood wrote that a national publication had listed *Manuscript* as the most important literary magazine in the United States and Rood found that praise rewarding. He assured Eudora Welty that many important publishers "watch our pages closely for new talent."

Rood's March 19, 1936, letter to Miss Welty accepting "Death of a Traveling Salesman" and "Magic" was long—two pages, single-spaced—and portrays Rood as a bright and eager editor who usually knew a good short story when he saw one. The policy of *Manuscript* was to publish stories in the order they arrived; by the usual method, Miss Welty's two stories would not have been in print until a year after their acceptance. Their quality, however, prompted an exception: "Death of a Traveling Salesman" appeared in the May–June 1936 issue and "Magic" in the September–October 1936 issue. Rood's enthusiasm was considerable. "Without any hesitation, we can say that DEATH OF A TRAVELING SALESMAN is one of the best stories that has come to our attention—and one of the best stories we have ever read.

It is superbly done. And MAGIC is only slightly short of it in quality. Needless to say we are excited over the stories, and over you—since you say these are the first two stories you have submitted."

In conjunction with publishing the stories, Rood had asked Miss Welty for biographical data, which she somewhat reluctantly supplied. On April 30, 1936, Rood wrote, "Yes, by all means, we do want a photograph of you. It is too late for the next issue, but we can use it when the other story appears. You did send a sort of sketch—at least information that we could and did use." What the Rood correspondence focused on, of course, was Miss Welty's fiction; however, brief discussion of his own artistic undertakings—piano, mural painting, and wood carvings—brought inquiries of interest from Miss Welty.[15] All in all, the circumstances surrounding Miss Welty's first short story publication were pleasant and encouraging; the appearance of the May–June 1936 issue of *Manuscript* was the modest launching of a great career. Frederick J. Hoffman has described "Death of a Traveling Salesman" as a story of amazing effectiveness, and Reynolds Price said it is the best story Miss Welty has ever written. Some critics would disagree with Price, but no one—including Miss Welty—will deny that her *first* published story remains a valuable and respected part of her work.

Other publications quickly followed. From 1937 to 1939, the *Southern Review* brought out six of Miss Welty's stories, and its editors, Robert Penn Warren and Cleanth Brooks, and business manager Albert Erskine, became staunch Welty supporters. These stories brought Miss Welty to the attention of Katherine Anne Porter. She in turn interested Ford Madox Ford, who praised Miss Welty's remarkable gift and predicted she would achieve great things. From 1936 to 1955, a burst of activity occurred, but the publications came after many earlier rejections. Charlotte Capers, former director of the Mis-

sissippi Department of Archives and History and long-
time friend of Miss Welty, has traced the precarious
history of "Petrified Man," which was rejected by an
editor of *Literary America*, by Robert Penn Warren of the
Southern Review, and by Arnold Gingrich of *Esquire*.[16]
Warren's rejection was dated January 13, 1937, but less
than a month later, he expressed regrets over the decision. By March of the next year, he asked for another
look at "Petrified Man," and six months later repeated his
request. The story finally did appear in the *Southern Review* in 1939, but just barely, since, as Charlotte Capers
reported, Miss Welty had burned the manuscript and
had to write the story a second time—from memory.

   "Petrified Man" was not the only Eudora Welty
story to suffer rejection. *Literary America* returned
"Shape in Air," "Flowers for Marjorie," and "Responsibility"; John Rood also had reservations about "Shape in
Air"; Brooks and Warren sent back "Flowers for Marjorie," "The Visit," "In the Station," "Sister," "The
Death of Miss Belle," "Acrobats in the Park," and
"Powerhouse," as well as verse which Warren found interesting but did not publish. In 1937 Harold Strauss of
Covici-Friede Publishers returned a manuscript of stories
and photographs which he claimed presented insur-
mountable difficulties for publication. His remarks echo
some of the reviews that later greeted Miss Welty's work.
Strauss saw that the stories clearly had merit, but the
charm they conveyed did not allay his reservations about
their vagueness, unfocused sensibility, and creation of
mood rather than plot. R. N. Linscott of Houghton Mif-
flin had similar complaints about "The Cheated."
Although Whit Burnett (*Story and the Story Press*) liked
"Keela, the Outcast Indian Maiden" and "Why I Live at
the P.O.," he still rejected these stories, which, along
with "Petrified Man" and "Powerhouse," have made their
way into the established Welty canon. Over the years,
Miss Welty has not dwelt on the stories that went out

and came back, but rather on the good fortune that so often has greeted her fiction. "I believe I've always been lucky," she remarked, "my work has always landed safely and among friends."[17]

When her work appeared not only in *Manuscript* but in the *Southern Review, Prairie Schooner, Accent,* and other magazines, a number of editors wrote urging her to produce a novel. It is that "venerable literary custom," Charles Poore has said, "which, if transferred to painting, would harass good easel-artists with demands that they go in for wall-wide murals; if transferred to sports, would urge champion hundred-yard runners to concentrate on the mile or the marathon."[18] By far the most important and fruitful response to Welty's appearance as a short story writer came from John Woodburn of Doubleday, Doran, who oversaw the publication of her first book—not a novel but a short story collection entitled *A Curtain of Green* (1941). The jovial and cordial relations between Miss Welty and Woodburn are reflected in their correspondence. With the collection in process, Woodburn wrote that he had "perjured myself and said that you were hard at work on a novel. Please save my immortal soul." In June 1940 Woodburn's letter turned poetic, and his call for a novel somewhat more desperate.

> Oh, the boys in the band
> And the boys at the bar,
> They don't understand
> When they ask where you are . . .
> I wonder if you
> Would come back if you knew
> THERE'S A TEAR IN MY BEER TONIGHT
>
> P.S. Will you please write a novel for me?
> P.P.S. Pretty Please?

By 1942, Doubleday, Doran had published Welty's short novel, *The Robber Bridegroom.* The longer works came, but not because various publishers and editors

relentlessly called for them. Eudora Welty follows her
own nature and talent and has insisted that she has never
written anything "that didn't spring naturally to mind
and engage my imagination."[19] When the novel suited,
she used that genre.

The details of Miss Welty's first association with a
major publishing house are interesting indeed, especially
her close relationship with John Woodburn. As publication of her short story collection neared, Woodburn
urged Miss Welty to be in New York around September
5 for a party "with ice cream and cake and Katherine M.
[sic] Porter." The party would be a "way of launching
you, like a boat. At the proper moment when the cameras
are ready I will break a bottle of Paul Roger—'14 over
your brow and we will send you down the ways." The
serious side of publishing A Curtain of Green is reflected
in Woodburn's praise: "The book is going to be very
handsome, and everyone in the state of Mississippi is
going to be very proud of you, but no one in the state of
Mississippi or any other of the forty-seven states will be
prouder than / Yours truly / John." Playful good spirits
emerged in Woodburn's letters, which carried such
greetings as "Eudora," "Hello Peaches," "Baby," "Dear
Little Friend," "Fate Malone, Baby," "Eudora Bull
Creecher," and "Eu," and frequently contained items
from his Humor Department. "I found a name for your
delight. It is the name of an author, a lady author, whose
efforts did not meet with our complete approval. Here is
the name. That is it. Right here: Mrs. Frasquita Single-
tary Overmire, Honest." Of special note is a handwritten
letter dated Thanksgiving Day, 1942, in which Woodburn announced his decision to leave Doubleday and join
Harcourt Brace. Particularly upset over the minimal
advertising Doubleday had done for Welty's short novel
The Robber Bridegroom (1942), Woodburn urged her to
ask Ken McCormick to release her from the option
Doubleday held and move with him to Harcourt. A long

letter from McCormick cited the disadvantages of leaving Doubleday, but Miss Welty asked for and received a formal option cancellation on December 15, 1942. Her letter clearly stated that personal loyalty to Woodburn as her editor and friend overrode any of her considerations.

In May 1943 Woodburn said that Harcourt would publish *The Wide Net and Other Stories* in the fall; in June he wrote in typical teasing fashion, "We gotta have galleys, gal. What tooken you so long?" By August, Woodburn had gotten fishnet and a starfish to decorate the Harcourt window displaying the book, and he wrote Miss Welty his hope "that you will be able to come to New York at that time and stand in the window, draped in fishnet, personally disposing of your books to the clamoring customers and giving a free starfish with each copy." Their admiration for each other was considerable, and Woodburn's humor in letter writing only underscored their mutual respect. In a June 7, 1943 letter, Woodburn slipped in some amusing couplets which still bring a smile: "The Bronte of the South, of the Black Belt she / Is the one and only, incomparable, Eudora Welty." After *The Wide Net*, Miss Welty's next book was *Delta Wedding* (1946), but by its publication date, John Woodburn had also left Harcourt. (He was next with Henry Holt, and finally with Little, Brown.) Miss Welty could not have given higher praise than she did in saying that Woodburn "was a wonderful editor, the same kind as Max Perkins; he cared about work for its own sake."[20]

Harcourt Brace published Miss Welty's books through *Thirteen Stories* (1965). However, between *The Bride of Innisfallen*, which appeared in 1955, and *Losing Battles*, at last scheduled to be published in 1970, a long interval had elapsed during which her only new work had been the juvenile one *The Shoe Bird* (1964). Everyone Miss Welty had known at Harcourt was gone, and when the firm's attitude toward the manuscript was not satisfactory, Diarmuid Russell asked Albert Erskine of

Random House to make an offer. His offer was accepted.
This move completed a circle, since Erskine had been
associated with the *Southern Review* when Miss Welty's
stories first began to appear.

A glance at the list of Eudora Welty's essays, sketches, and critical reviews reveals her far-reaching interests.
For example, "Is There a Reader in the House?" (*Mississippi Education Advance*, November 1955) expressed concern over children reading so little: "You hate to see a
whole world of pleasure and excitement and wisdom and
glory go lost, its very existence unsuspected." Her advice
to prospective young writers was to look at their own
experience and to READ. In "The Right To Read" (*Mississippi Magic*, May 1961), Miss Welty urged improve-
ments in library offerings in state penal institutions and
mental hospitals. Her contribution to the fiftieth
anniversary celebration of the Lamar Life Insurance
Company emphasized place and blood ties, elements significant in her fiction.

It is partly a sort of kinship, a blood-tie, the thing that is thicker
than water. Most of all, though, it is the passionate and guiding
belief my father instilled in me of the meaning of the "home
company"—the integrity of a thing that springs from and lives
on its own nourishing soil. And regardless of how we may grow
and come to link up with a larger world, a natural process of
development, it is the principle of that first "goodness," that
original integrity, that must be the root of all excellence that
can follow, and will always responsibly account for it and bless
it.

Involvements with the theater range from musical
sketches for revues at the Phoenix Theater to the stage
adaptations of *The Robber Bridegroom* and *The Ponder
Heart*. The most ambitious attempt at a musical was
What Year Is This?, which Miss Welty wrote in collabora-
tion with Hildegard Dolson. "See Your Analyst Twice a
Year" and "Perfume Case" were among Miss Dolson's
contributions to the revue, and Miss Welty's song on *The*

New York Times ran, in part, "I can read all day / In Society's blurb / who married whom / In which suburb."[21] Particularly interesting is Miss Welty's "Fifty-Seventh Street Rag-Ballet," which opens in a Fifty-seventh Street art gallery and satirizes "arty" trends. Bewildered by what he sees, an old man laments, "Where oh where / Are the nudes of yesteryear," with no apology to Villon. The "Grandma Moses faction" fared none too well either:

> My little pretties of doers in dimity've
> Done right well. That's American Primitive.
> Sonny, it's as homey as cheese and crackers,
> I can let you have it for a thousand smackers.
> Just as old fashioned as Ring-around-the-Rosey—
> Nobody puts the blinkers on Grandma Mosey.

A note accompanying this sketch indicates that the ballet was to be taken seriously: "The ballet is primarily a beautiful one. It utilizes, with as much imagination as desired, the kinds and varieties of modern painting as well as the kinds of people connected with a modern gallery." The most successful of Miss Welty's contributions was a clever skit, "Bye-Bye Brevoort," which was included in *The Littlest Revue* during the 1955–56 Phoenix Theater season. *What Year Is This?* kept Miss Welty and Hildegard Dolson busy writing an entire summer in New York, but Lehman Engle, another Jacksonian, read it and predicted it would come to nothing because the work had no blackout. Whatever the reason, the musical in toto never reached the stage, but "it was a wonderful excuse to see all the shows on Broadway that season."[22]

Miss Welty worked with John Robinson on the screenplay of *The Robber Bridegroom* and agreed to let Eddie Dowling see the script when he set out to prepare a stage version. So that Dowling could get the feel of the wild and rugged country around Rodney's Landing, Miss Welty sent him a few snapshots. The stage adaptation, however, was finally done by Alfred Uhry and Robert Waldman. After a short visit to Jackson to absorb local color, Jerome Chodorov and Joseph Fields brought their adaptation of *The Ponder Heart* to a successful Broadway run, with David Wayne as Uncle Daniel and Una Merkel in her Tony Award-winning role of Edna Earle. However, the Chodorov and Fields adaptation made serious changes in the original, changes Miss Welty challenged in a letter to the authors and in notations on their script. In spite of the New York success, Miss Welty felt much closer to the Jackson New Stage production of *The Ponder Heart*. "That seemed mine, and it was an entirely different feeling."[23]

Alice Parker of New York City is completing a musical version of *The Ponder Heart* which is best described as an opera bouffe. It promises to be a lively and thoroughly delightful production. The work (Miss Welty is pleased with the libretto) retains Edna Earle as narrator (a role for mezzo-soprano) and is scheduled for presentation in April, 1982, at Eastern Mennonite University, as part of a Eudora Welty program to be held in Harrisonburg, Virginia.

Other dramatizations included a New Stage production of "A Season of Dreams," an original presentation based on selected works. In 1968 Emily Evans staged adaptations of "A Piece of News" and "Petrified Man" at the Eldred Theater, Western Reserve University, and the Jackson Ballet Guild sold out its City Auditorium for the April 20, 1968, world premiere of "The Shoe Bird," Miss Welty's children's book. In 1980, Brenda Currin starred in a one woman show, "Sister and Miss Lexie," an introduction to the world of Eudora Welty, which ran at the Chelsea Theater Cabaret in New York City. The dramatizing and the televising of Welty's dialogue stories have been natural steps, and when she herself reads a story in public, the occasion is never a mere reading, but a performance.

Since 1942, Eudora Welty has been a frequent reviewer and essayist, primarily in *The New York Times Book Review*, the *Saturday Review*, the *Hudson Review*, and the *Sewanee Review*. Her subjects have ranged from "Africa and Paris and Russia" (three books of photographs) and "For the Window-Box Farmer" (a review of *Enjoy Your House Plants*), to *The Western Journals of Washington Irving*, edited by John Francis McDermott. Perceptive, shrewd, and appreciative are words that characterize her critical work, as well as her lectures at colleges and universities. An introduction to *Hanging by a Thread*, an anthology of thirty-three suspense stories edited by Joan Kahn, shows not only Miss Welty's appreciation of the suspense story, but also her judgment of suspense as a writing device: "Suspense, *per se*, is of not too much account. Painful, pleasurable, or no opinion, suspense by itself is to a reader sensation only. It has one positive quality, duration." Even two cookbooks have Welty introductions: *The Jackson Cookbook* (1971) and *The Southern Hospitality Cookbook* (1976). In the latter, Miss Welty recalls the scene "when Jane Austen's Miss Bates, attending Mr. Weston's ball, is seated at the supper, she surveys the table with a cry, 'How shall we ever recollect half of the dishes?' When I sit down to Sunday dinner at Winifred's [the cookbook author] I feel like Miss Bates. What guest could not?"

In the 1930s, when Miss Welty worked for WPA, she began taking photographs for her own pleasure. Since the family car was not available for her weekday picture-taking trips, she had to catch rides or go by train or bus and could not always stop for appealing subjects when she wished. Most of the photographs—buildings, street scenes, rural life, and unposed studies of Mississippi blacks—remain unpublished.[24] As early as 1935, Miss Welty made serious attempts to have the photographs published, but met with little success. Harrison Smith praised her excellent work in "Black Saturday," and regretted that his firm decided against accepting it: he did not think they could overcome the competition of Julia Peterkin's 1933 volume, *Roll, Jordan, Roll*, and the sluggish book market that resulted from the economic woes of the 1930s. Photographic Galleries in New York City did present an exhibit of forty-five Welty photographs in 1936, including "Bird Pageant," "The Bottle Tree," "Tomato Packers, Recess," "House-boat on Pearl River," and "Madonna with Coca-Cola." In 1971, when a book of ninety-eight photographs, *One Time, One Place*, did at long last appear, Miss Welty's introduction confirmed the importance of her photographs—the process of taking those pictures was one of discarding innocence for experience, of discovering not only the hard time of the Depression in the rural South, but also of seeing the story of life in the faces of the people:

I learned from my own pictures, one by one, and had to; for I think we are the breakers of our own hearts. I learned quickly enough when to click the shutter, but what I was becoming aware of more slowly was a story-writer's truth: the thing to wait on, to reach there in time for, is the moment in which people reveal themselves. You have to be ready, in yourself; you have to know the moment when you see it.

Exhibits of Miss Welty's photographs have shown their relationship to her fiction, but the visually minded can see into the stories without photographic aid, as a brief passage from "Kin" illustrates. In the first section of the story, Rachael, the black servant, has established her role as a conscientious and thoughtful individual, particularly solicitous of Kate's mother Ethel, who is ill. Rachael has "in her stately way" delivered a letter from Sister Anne, selected the big shell dish for the city candy Dicey brought, baked a Lady Baltimore cake, and, because Dicey and Kate forgot to get the roses early when they should have been cut, gathered them in the heat of the day. Her thoughts are for Ethel's sick room and her actions are punctuated with brisk movements: she entered *bearing* a vaseful of roses, *paraded* them through the room and around the bed, and setting them on the table *marched* back to her kitchen, her deed carried out with ceremony. As the cousins, Dicey and Kate, leave for Mingo to visit great-uncle Felix, they go, taking Rachael's treasures, dispossessing her. Dicey and the reader see Rachael in a pose fit for a camera—alone, her efforts for this household taken to another one without a word to her. "Around the house, as we climbed with our loads into the car, I saw Rachael looking out from the back hall window, with her cheek in her hand. She watched us go, carrying off her cake and her flowers too."

Miss Welty's stories, novels, essays, reviews, lectures, introductions, and dramatic work mark her as a true Woman of Letters. Her concerted efforts in fiction are complemented by her other writing: in all her work the reader finds the celebration of life, concern for the individual, and incomparable technical skill. Hers is a rich and rewarding career, filled, as she has said, with "great descents of good fortune."

2

~·~·~·~·~·~·~·~·~·~·~·~·~·~·~·~·~·~·

The Prism of Comedy

A consideration of the comic element in Eudora Welty must include almost all of her work, but it is often true that Miss Welty's way of being comic is a serious one. While the comic is a major element, individual works must also be examined from other perspectives. The comic aspects in *Losing Battles*, for example, are foremost; nevertheless, it must also be read as a serious commentary on rural family life, on the uphill struggle to educate those who do not wish to learn, on the sacrifices that love requires. This chapter gives particular emphasis to the comic element in Welty; subsequent ones treat the major works (except *The Ponder Heart*) in other ways, attempting to point out different thematic and stylistic concerns and to treat them as the serious works of fiction that they are.

On October 29, 1946, Lambert Davis (then an editor at Harcourt Brace) answered Miss Welty's request for copies of two classics of American humor—Judge Augustus Baldwin Longstreet's *Georgia Scenes* (1835) and Joseph Glover Baldwin's *The Flush Times of Alabama and Mississippi* (1853).

I think we have located a copy of Longstreet's *Georgia Scenes* for you, and I hope to send you the volume some time this week. The Baldwin book is proving more elusive, but I have our hounds out on several trails. I think you will enjoy both books, and I will be very eager to hear from you what you think of

them. There is a part of your writing self that is of Longstreet-
Baldwin descent, though you may be as embarrassed by such a
cousinly comparison as you were in your childhood by similar
comparisons that your aunts and uncles made.[1]

One has only to read *The Robber Bridegroom* to see traces
of Longstreet and Baldwin, and Miss Welty bears many
cousinly comparisons with other strains of American
humor. Although she herself has not written an essay
solely devoted to the subject of humor, comments scat-
tered throughout her critical writing give signals that she
is a master of the comic mode.

As Elizabeth Bowen remarked to Charles Ritchie,
when Miss Welty begins talking, she is very funny indeed—the strain of comedy a part of her nature. "The
Radiance of Jane Austen" (included in *The Eye of the Story*)
is an excellent starting place to discern much about Miss
Welty's attitude toward fiction, the comic in particular.
She praised Jane Austen, saying that "habit of mind of
seeing both sides of her own subject—of seeing it indeed
in the round—is a little unusual . . . to writers and
readers of our day." To see in the round focuses the
writer on the serious as well as the comic, the satiric
word in humorous guise, the endless incongruities that
create humor. Jane Austen saw her subject in the round,
but Miss Welty contends our century does not: "Ours is
the century of unreason, the stamp of our behavior is
violence or isolation: non-meaning is looked upon with
some solemnity; and for the purpose of writing novels,
most human behavior is looked at through the frame, or
the knot-hole, of alienation." Above all, the writer of
comedy must be a highly conscious artist; indeed, each of
Jane Austen's novels "is a formidable engine of strategy."
The elements of comedy are not ephemeral, nor are they
isolated from the whole. An unaging delight is the exuberance Austen's youthful characters possess; her
novels themselves come to us intact: over the years "the
gaiety of the novels has pervaded them, the irony has

kept its bite, the reasoning is still sweet, the sparkle un-
diminished." The knothole of alienation would never
serve the writer of comedy: "Comedy is sociable and
positive, and exacting. Its methods, its boundaries, its
point, all belong to the familiar." The imagery of whole-
ness, sparkle, radiance, and exuberance coalesce when
Miss Welty says of Jane Austen's work, "A clear ray of
light strikes full upon the scene, resulting in the prism of
comedy."

In her essay on the English novelist Henry Green,
Miss Welty provides a definition of sorts: "Humor is not
a relief, as beauty is not a decoration; all that can be said
is that there occur, when these qualities appear, highly
sensitive spots where you are surest to hear the pulsebeat
of the fiction." The humor must be intrinsic within stories themselves; it must be, as Miss Welty said in reviewing Faulkner's *Intruder in the Dust*, "as much their blood
and bone as the passion and poetry." Indeed, in Faulkner's "Spotted Horses" she found that "in all that shining
fidelity to place lies the heart and secret of this tale's
comic glory." Chekhov embraced many of the concerns
southern writers have shared and written of—individual-
ity, the sense of family, and a sense of fate overtaking
life; in addition, Miss Welty sees Chekhov's Russian
humor akin to the humor of a southerner. It is the kind
that lies primarily in character—everybody talking, nobody listening, everybody tolerant of each other's
idiosyncrasies. Such humor shows forth in much of Miss
Welty's fiction, especially in *Losing Battles*, where the
narration required a different technique for her since
little was explained, evaluated, or described by the authorial voice. "I tried to see if I could make everything
shown, brought forth, without benefit of the author's
telling any more about what was going on inside the
characters' minds and hearts. For me, this makes almost
certainly for comedy."[2]

The range of Miss Welty's comic devices includes

many that are traditional in American humor. Disingenuous characters like Huckleberry Finn provide humor that stems from the disparity between the character's and the reader's understanding and judgment. Unaware of the humor she creates, Leota (in "Petrified Man") sees nothing amiss in announcing to her ten o'clock shampoo-and-set customer, "Honey, them goobers has been in my purse a week if they's been in it a day." Utterly puzzled by his wife's suicide note, William Wallace Jamison (in "The Wide Net") labors the point to his matter-of-fact friend Virgil. Since Hazel was in mortal fear of water, William Wallace cannot understand how she could kill herself by jumping into the river to drown. Virgil's explanation is deadpan: "Jumped backward. Didn't look."

Walter Blair and Hamlin Hill in *American Humor: From Poor Richard to Doonesbury*, note that "stretchers" were the essence of early American humor; and many of Miss Welty's comic characters fall with ease into stretching or exaggerating, especially Edna Earle, that indefatigable narrator of *The Ponder Heart*. Having described herself as "a great reader that never has time to read," she contradicts herself, claiming to have read *The House of a Thousand Candles* for the thousandth time. With Narciss at the wheel of the Studebaker, Uncle Daniel and Bonnie Dee Peacock, a clerk from Woolworth's, end up in Silver City to be married. Disgruntled over this unexpected turn of events, Edna Earle laments that Silver City "was the only spot in Creation they could have gone to without finding somebody that knew enough to call Clay 123 and I'd answer." From the details Edna Earle presents about the Peacock family's eating, the reader expects plump rather than pencil-slim characters, but she stretches things when she says Mrs. Peacock "was big and fat as a row of pigs." Leota exaggerates about recounting her love life to Mrs. Pike in "Petrified Man"—"I tole her ever'thing about ever'thing, from now on back to I don't know when—to when I first started goin' out."

One of *many* exaggerations in *Losing Battles* comes when
Jack Renfro explains away the fallen tree that blocks the
truck. "It was old and ready to fall. Lady May [not quite
two years old] could've pushed it over with her little
finger."

Like such Ring Lardner characters as the barber in
"Haircut," Gullible in *Gullible's Travels, Etc.*, Jack Keefe
in *You Know Me, Al*, and Fred Gross in *Own Your Own
Home*, many of Miss Welty's comic narrators expose their
warped natures as they disingenuously relate their deeds.
While pathos and tragedy often follow close behind the
comedy, her characters seldom are callous toward the
feelings of others or indifferent to the well-being of family and friends (as Lardner's can be), although characters
in "Petrified Man" and "Why I Live at the P.O." come
close to viciousness. Her fiction never approaches the
bitterness Mark Twain and many contemporary writers
share—frustration over the damned human race. Intent
on celebration, Eudora Welty's comic characters perpetu-
ate family history by telling its stories and by participat-
ing in weddings, reunions, and funerals. Through these
words and actions, they keep the past part of the present.

Homely figures of speech are staples throughout
Miss Welty's fiction, and often the comparisons are
amusing. Uncle Daniel cannot handle money and "giving
it to him would be like giving matches to a child." The
strange Spanish guitarist in "Music from Spain" flexed
his long fingers along his thighs "like a cat testing her
claws on a cushion." In *Losing Battles*, Ralph Renfro holds
up halves of a freshly cut melon "like the Tablets of the
Ten Commandments." Brother Bethune, the preacher
who proves to be a disappointment, gets a surge of energy when talk drifts to Judgment Day, a time, he declares, when "Banner Cemetery is going to be throwed
open like a hill of potatoes." In "The Bride of Innisfallen," a schoolgirl joins others in the train compartment
and her hat "hid her bent head like a candle snuffer."

The somewhat mysterious lady in this group smoothed down her raincoat "with a rattle like the reckless slamming of bureau drawers." The sometime exhibitionist in "June Recital," Mr. Voight, "ran up the steps with a sound like a green stick along a fence." King MacLain, that Zeus-Casanova, appears in "Sir Rabbit" standing "on top of the gully, wearing a yellowy Panama hat and a white linen suit with the sleeves as ridgy as two washboards."

When literal-minded characters, for whatever reason, bring up inconvenient facts, they are silenced, and the resulting humor has an overtone of seriousness. Mr. Pike reminds his wife that their former landlord, Mr. Petrie, had extended them neighborly favors, but Mrs. Pike (intent on collecting the reward for this criminal) bluntly says, "You can go to hell, Canfield." In *Delta Wedding*, one of the old aunts will not listen to the wedding photographer's narration about the train death of the young girl Ellen and George had encountered. Before details can be given, she demands, "Change the subject." A chorus of protests greets Nathan Beecham at the reunion in *Losing Battles*, when he tries to tell his shameful deed of the past.

Comic migrations, the mixing of different social levels by moving characters from one region to another, occur as a major device in *The Ponder Heart*, *Losing Battles*, and *The Optimist's Daughter*. The murder trial of Daniel Ponder has often been described as splendid comedy and as a jolt to the entire judicial system. Part of the comedy comes from the victim's family, the Peacocks, who have traveled from Polk to Clay for the trial. Edna Earle is sure that more of the family has showed up for Uncle Daniel's trial than showed up for Bonnie Dee's funeral; their mode of transportation, a pick-up truck. Amusing details of their dress and behavior quickly show the reader that the Peacocks are socially unacceptable to Clay residents. Mrs. Peacock wears new bedroom slippers with pompoms on the toes, and Mr. Peacock (face as red as a Tom turkey and not a tooth in his head) has on a new pair of pants—the tag still sticks out of one seam. Johnnie Rae Peacock is decked out in her dead sister's "telephone-putting-in costume—very warm for June." Taking up two rows in the courtroom, the Peacocks are all sizes and ages; they sit with gaping mouths and constantly go to the water fountain, which stopped working years ago. When court is interrupted while Miss Edna Earle's girl takes count for dinner at the Beulah Hotel, the Peacocks do not raise their hands, since they have brought theirs— and all the dogs as well. Rather than listening to the testimony, Mrs. Peacock talks through the trial, asking about churches in Clay and seeking remedies for her swollen finger joints. Sporadically, Old Man Peacock rises to ask if anyone has a timepiece. The daughters sit in a row, the eight-year-old brother walks up and down the aisle with a harmonica in his breathing mouth, and babies slide to the floor making straightway for the door. Treva chews gum. It is true that all the residents of Clay at the trial perform antics of their own, but the Peacock clan, away from home and out of place, sparks exceptional humor.

A comic migration in *Losing Battles* takes a different form—through a series of mishaps, Judge and Mrs. Moody join a lower social group, the numerous relatives at the Beecham reunion. Part of the comedy arises from the Moodys' discomfort at being thrust not only among total strangers, but into the bosom of a family whose peerless son Jack was sentenced to the penitentiary at Parchman by the same Judge Moody who now accepts their hospitality. The vast social separation between families is given first by contrasting their types of transportation: the Moodys have a fancy Buick (stalled now and perched precariously on Banner Top), while Jack's family has had to sell his prized possession—the train-wrecked, rebuilt Coca-Cola truck. The babbling

Beechams and Renfros may have some differences
among themselves, but to an outside force they present a
rather united front—and the numerical odds are clearly
against the Moodys. Unable to alter their situation,
Judge Moody wedges into the last available seat—a
school chair—and admonishes his wife: "Just eat like everybody else, Maud Eva. It can't be helped." Then he
"set his teeth into a big chicken back."

Everything about the Moodys marks them as outsiders and when Gloria (Jack's wife) spies them, she declares: "Their faces stick out of a crowd at me like four-
leafs in a clover path." Invited to relate the family history, Brother Bethune, the Baptist preacher, falls by the
wayside, but recovers by elaborately introducing the two
visitors who have already been sitting on the porch for
some time. His absurd words and logic mark him a true
comic character; the deadpan responses from the Moodys
underscore their bewilderment.

"Well, let me welcome a surprise visitor to our midst!" Brother
Bethune called. "Judge Oscar Moody, of our county seat of
Ludlow! Let's all see him stand and take a bow! I know he's as
happy as I am to see where he's found himself today. And the
lady setting in front of him is none other than his good wife and
helpmeet. Stand up, Mrs. Judge! I wasn't fixing to get me a
wife till I finished hunting, and still without a wife to this day,"
he turned around and said to his gun.

"Why did we stand up?" Judge Moody asked his wife.

"I normally stand up when it's asked of me," she said.
"Now, we can sit down." She sat.

Further consternation ensues as the family enters
into a frantic discussion of forgiveness and Judge Moody
stubbornly resists being forgiven. The climax of this
banter comes as Aunt Birdie grandly forgives Judge
Moody for pronouncing sentence on Jack. His futile protest—"I don't want your forgiveness for being a fair

judge at a trial. I don't deserve *that*"—is quickly met by Miss Beulah's non sequitur—"Don't tell me, sir, you have nothing to be forgiven for, I'm his mother." Education, dress, and vocabulary settle the Moodys in their social class, but like it or not, the Judge becomes part of the reunion. Miss Beulah asks, "Are you trying to tell us you come into this story too?" He does indeed, as he reads the last requests of their mutual teacher, Miss Julia Mortimer, requests written in pencil around the page edges of her spelling-book, and the Judge also reads the letter Miss Julia had sent to him (written, Maud Eva realizes from its gold edge, on the fly leaf of the Bible). Aunt Birdie voices a common protest: "I can't understand it when he reads it to us. Can't he just tell it?" Accustomed as they are to their own voices retelling familiar stories, the reading of formal writing falls strangely on their ears. Aunt Birdie complains she can not understand the long words in the letter (the longest are "survival instinct," "desperation," "encourage," "memory," and "reliable"), and Judge Moody retorts in disbelief: "What long words?" Not even Gloria, Miss Julia's fallen protégé, responds to the sadness of the teacher's death as deeply as does Judge Moody. Various reflections about Miss Julia reveal the comic character of those who voice them. Mr. Renfro recalls that when Miss Julia boarded with them, she read in the daytime, an activity he found "surpassing strange for a well woman to do." Uncle Percy and Uncle Dolphus resent the request from the spelling-book will that they attend the funeral— "I ain't a-going. . . . Now what's she going to do about it?" Uncle Noah Webster (who shares none of *the* Noah Webster's virtues) remembers Miss Julia's voice. "She had a might of sweetness and power locked up in her voice. To waste it on teaching was a sin." When the chatter eases into another subject, Judge Moody speaks his melancholy line, "It could make a stone cry," which he utters not only over the contents of Miss Julia's will and letter and upon the unspeakable indignation she endured during her last illness, but also on the imperceptive comments Beechams and Renfros have made. As funny as the long scene is, bitterness and pathos emerge. As touching as the Judge's line is, it is undercut by Mrs. Moody's anticlimactic remark about his association with Julia Mortimer. "Yet you vow it was all platonic?" To which the Judge curtly replies, "Don't try to read any secrets into this, Maud Eva."

The Optimist's Daughter has two comic migrations. In the first, the Dalzell family from Fox Hill, Mississippi, are gathered in a New Orleans hospital waiting room during the aftermath of Mr. Dalzell's operation. "His chances are a hundred to one against." The family group consists of the old woman, its official spokesman, five or six grown men who resemble her and are apparently her brothers, the wizened daughter, and the youngest daughter. Their coats lie piled on a table; shoe boxes and paper sacks which had contained their supper lie empty on the floor. Since the sick man is in intensive care, family members take turns for the brief visits allowed. Then Archie Lee refuses to go in, takes refuge in the pint bottle of whiskey he has, and soon goes to sleep on the sofa, the bottle dropping from his relaxed hand to the floor. Wanda Fay, whose husband, Judge McKelva, has undergone eye surgery, is instantly at home with the Dalzells and joins them in "vying and trouble-swapping." The Dalzell clan manufactures waiting-room laughter as they vow they will get water into their dying father should he be denied it. Completely unaware of any impropriety in their behavior, the Dalzells exhibit in public—amid nurses and doctors—all the antics inherent in their nature. Laurel McKelva Hand, the judge's daughter and a fabric designer from Chicago, has nothing in common with the Dalzells or with Wanda Fay, whom her father has recently married. Obliged to share the hospital waiting room with them all, Laurel sees their

somewhat vulgar but amusing behavior and gives them
"the wide berth of her desolation."

In the second comic migration, the Chisoms of Ma-
drid, Texas, journey to Mount Salus, Mississippi, in a
pick-up truck to attend the funeral of Wanda Fay's husband. The trip, Bubba announces to anyone who will
listen, took eight hours, they crossed the river at Vicks-
burg, and they will have to turn around and go right
back. They have not come dressed in customary funeral
clothes. Bubba, who is to be a pallbearer, wears a windbreaker, and seven-year-old Wendell has on a cowboy
suit replete with hat and pistol holders. Since Wanda Fay
has not yet come downstairs, the Chisoms are amid
strangers (Major Bullock "summoned" them, but has
never met them) and in a house full of fine old furniture
that Fay's redecorating has not yet disposed of. Their
conversation comes naturally to them, with no thought
of its inappropriateness. Learning from Mrs. Pease the
brief details of Phillip Hand's death, Mrs. Chisom says
to Laurel, "So you ain't got father, mother, brother,
sister, husband, chick nor child. Not a soul to call on,
that's you." Then Mrs. Chisom relates the story of her
son Roscoe's suicide (stuffed windows and the door and
turned on all four eyes of the stove and the oven), taking
comfort that "he didn't do nothing any more serious to
harm his good looks." When Grandpa Chisom arrives by
bus from Bigbee, Mrs. Chisom drags him to Judge
McKelva's coffin and says, "Out of curiosity, who does
he remind you of?" Mercifully, Grandpa, the soul of
dignity, says "nobody," or Mrs. Chisom would doubt-
less be off on another tale of death, illness, or suicide. At
last, Wanda Fay, glistening in black satin, appears. Her
display over the coffin, "Hon, get up out of there," is in
character, but does not equal Mrs. Chisom's behavior
when her husband was buried. ("They couldn't hold me
half so easy. I tore up the whole house, I did.") The
Chisoms are well pleased with all aspects of the funeral:

the coffin was a fine one; burial was in the *new* part of the cemetery adorned with plastic flowers and overlooking the highway; the crowd was large without even counting the blacks; and Wanda Fay had had the good sense to break down at the right time. "You try begging sympathy later on, when folks has gone back about their business, and they don't appreciate your tears then. It just tries their nerves." The old-guard Mount Salus friends and neighbors have their own peculiar quirks at the funeral, but safe in their home territory and social position, they are appalled and taken aback at the Texas Chisoms turned loose. When Major Bullock, tipsy as usual, steps forward to claim responsibility for having summoned Wanda Fay's kin, his wife mutters, "You just forgot to warn *us*." The funeral done, Mrs. Chisom inspects the large, roomy McKelva home with an eye worthy of Eliza Gant, and suggests that Wanda Fay would do well to convert it into a boarding house with her mama as the cook. Miss Tennyson Bullock recoils with "Great Day in the Morning!" The Chisoms' antic behavior is ironically juxtaposed with the mourning for Judge McKelva and with Laurel's emotion at having now to leave behind the home of her youth. Their lack of taste and manners is extreme. At the buffet after the funeral, Bubba comes away with both hands around a ham sandwich. Leaving, Mrs. Chisom declares she "wouldn't mind taking some of that ham along . . . if it's just going begging." Their conversation, dress, habits, and style do not meet the expectations of Miss Tennyson Bullock, but Wanda Fay's family is just what she says—not hypocrites.

Although Miss Welty views comedy as sociable, positive, and exacting, some of her characters engage in deeds and conversations that are not light-hearted and arouse laughter only with an accompanying shock. Some episodes can be described as black humor, which "discovers cause for laughter in what has generally been regarded as too serious for frivolity: the death of man, the disintegration of social institutions, mental and physical disease, deformity, suffering, anguish, privation, and terror."[3] Although more prevalent since World War I, black humor has surfaced briefly whenever time provides distance.[4] In "Clytie," varying degrees of mental distress plague Clytie Farr, her sister Octavia, and her brother Gerald—remnants of the once prominent family for whom the town Farr's Gin was named. Clytie in her wanderings about takes no account of a driving rain, and ladies in town watch the drenched figure as her straw hat from the furnishing store sags on each side until it looks "like an old bonnet on a horse." Clytie herself makes no move to seek shelter until someone tells her to. She then turns and runs up the street, creating a ridiculous picture as she goes, "sticking out her elbows like chicken wings." Octavia, the tyrannical sister above stairs, has thick hair (grown back after an illness) dyed almost purple, and Gerald lives in a barricaded room with his whiskey. Their isolation is almost total except for Mr. Bobo, who comes regularly, but reluctantly, to shave the paralyzed father. Clytie's longings for acceptance and love lead to her death, an event at once pathetic and ludicrous. "When Old Lethy found her, she had fallen forward into the [rain] barrel, with her poor ladylike black-stockinged legs upended and hung apart like a pair of tongs."

Maureen Fairchild (*Delta Wedding*), retarded daughter of the dead family hero Denis and the mad Virgie Lee, is not funny in a conventional sense. Difficult to contend with, Maureen provides a grim humor with her labored speech pattern and her inability to judge respective values. Marmion, one of the Fairchild houses on the plantation, is Maureen's by inheritance, but Dabney, the bride of *Delta Wedding*, would like to live in it. Casually, Dabney says to Maureen, "Look, honey—will you give your house to me?" and Maureen is quite agreeable. "You can have my house-la, and a bite-la of my apple too." The house is as easy to give away as the bite of apple. Not always so generous, Maureen leaps on top of the woodpile and, after a strange pause, pushes it over on Laura, the visiting cousin. Maureen feels no remorse and merely says incongruously, "Choo choo," and runs away. Geneva, one of the county orphans at camp in "Moon Lake," watches the attempts to revive the nearly drowned Easter and asks, "If Easter's dead, I get her coat for winter, all right." Practical considerations for her override concern or grief. In another grim episode, Aunt Nanny (*Losing Battles*) *grins* as she relates the dreadful story of being abandoned in infancy. "Well, listen— mothers come different. Mama had two, and gave away both of 'em, me and my sister, when we was squallers, and she didn't need to at all—it just suited her better. She's up the road with Papa now, busy living to a ripe old age." Nanny bypasses the difficulties the desertion must have caused.

Several female characters are adept at uttering taste- less remarks. In "Kin" Sister Anne flutters through the day as the itinerant photographer snaps pictures of half the county, using the parlor at Mingo as a studio. Oper- ating on excitement, Sister Anne is more interested in the cake and roses Dicey and Kate have brought than in their visit. When the girls ask where their ailing great- uncle Felix has been moved, they get no quick answer. "Where have you got him put?" In response, Sister Anne launches into the details of the photographer and his clients, slipping into the middle of her remarks a cryptic answer about Felix: "Got him put back out of all the commotion." Before she will lead them to Felix, she must find out what kind of cake they have brought and lick a fingerful of icing, exclaim over Dicey's engagement ring, and stick "the roses into a smoky glass vase too small for them into which she'd run too little water." At last they find Felix, housed in a backroom Dicey never thought was taken seriously as part of the house. His transfer was accomplished, Sister Anne blithely says, with some help from the blacks, "but it was mostly my fat little self." As best she can recall, she gained Uncle Felix's consent by telling him a story. Her free photograph is worth more than all the family's comforts.

Aunt Cleo in *Losing Battles* bears some resemblance to Sister Anne, but is far more insensitive and crude. Recently married to Noah Webster Beecham, Cleo does not know the family secrets or connections, and through her frequent questions the reader pieces together much information. When Miss Beulah warns the family not to spoil Jack's homecoming by telling him his truck is gone, Aunt Cleo comments, "But a truck? How did Jack ever get hold of such a scarcity to start with? . . . You-all don't look like you was ever that well-fixed." Indeed, the Renfros are not well-fixed, but the extravagance of a new tin roof and the abundance of the reunion dinner are brave attempts to forestall the bleak economic truth. The attempts are lost on Cleo. Several family members later take up the history of the truck, a Coca-Cola delivery truck driven by Ears Broadwee and hit broadside by a train. Maud Eva Moody shows no concern or compassion, only dismay, that the Coca-Cola people hire such careless drivers. Aunt Cleo (who does not yet know Ears survived without a scratch) hears Aunt Nanny claim the Broadwees as kin, but still says with her customary coldness, "I reckon there wasn't enough left of him for you-all to pick up and bury. Have his funeral with a sealed coffin?"

Nathan Beecham, haunted by guilt (he let a sawmill black hang for a murder he himself committed), has cut off his right hand in expiation, and spends his lonely life wandering along the road, placing signs that call sinners to repentance. He spends with his family only the day and night of the annual reunion, mortifying himself further by always standing up and by refusing to eat. His sister Beulah urges him not to be so hard on himself, but

Nathan remains in the agony of his conscience. Cleo, however, callously says, "Hey! Ain't that a play hand?"

Uncle Nathan's still uplifted right hand was lineless and smooth, pink as talcum. It had no articulation but looked caught forever in a pose of picking up a sugar lump out of the bowl. On its fourth, most elevated finger was a seal ring.

"How far up does it go?" asked Aunt Cleo.

"It's just exactly as far as what you see that ain't real," said Miss Beulah. "That hand come as a present from all his brothers, and his sister supplied him the ring for it. Both of 'em takes off together. Satisfied?"

"For now," Aunt Cleo said, as they all went back to their seats.

Her satisfaction over this issue lasts until the album is passed and an early photo of Nathan is identified. "Well, he's got both hands," Aunt Cleo challenged them. "Was he born like you and I?"

Church-affiliated characters are rather scarce in Miss Welty's fiction, and when they turn out to be preachers—Brother Bethune in *Losing Battles*, Mr. Dustan Renfro, the Methodist preacher in *Delta Wedding*, the two red-headed Baptist preachers in *The Ponder Heart*, Mr. Carson in "Lily Daw and the Three Ladies," or Dr. Bolt in *The Optimist's Daughter*—they are either ridiculous or ineffective. Preachers' wives are meddlesome, silly, and curious about sex. Mrs. Carson, along with Etta Watts and Aimee Slocum, campaigns to save Lily Daw (who is not bright) from the possibility of any sexual encounters by shipping her off to the mental institution at Ellisville. When Lily announces she is going to marry the xylophone player from the traveling show and was with him last night, the women become slightly hysterical. Mrs. Carson asks, "Tell me, Lily—just yes or no—are you the same as you were?" Convinced that the xylophone player is only "after Lily's body," Mrs. Car-

son sees little profit in dragging him back even at gun-
point to marry Lily. When Lily prefers marriage to Ellisville, Mrs. Carson explains: "We've all asked God, Lily
. . . and God seemed to tell us—Mr. Carson, too—that
the place where you ought to be, so as to be happy,
was Ellisville." Lily looks "reverent but stubborn." A
bribe—her hope chest filled with new treasures—sets
things in motion for Ellisville, but the xylophone player
suddenly appears and marriage now becomes the goal.
This second change in plans upsets Lily, but Mrs. Carson whispers, "Hush, and we'll all have some ice-cream
cones later," and goes off to call her husband. "I can get
him here in five minutes: I know exactly where he is."

In a much later work, *The Optimist's Daughter* (1972),
Judge McKelva's body lies in state at his home, and Mrs.
Bolt, the minister's wife, elbows her way in to see, "as if
Judge McKelva's body were the new baby." Her words
to Laurel concern food, not grief and death. "And here
I'd been waiting to see who it was I was saving my
Virginia ham for. . . . It's headed right for your kitchen."
When Laurel returns from the cemetery, Mrs. Bolt
greets her with "So you see? Here's the Virginia ham!"
Then "as if everything had turned out all right: she
offered a little red rag of it on a Ritz cracker. Then she
scampered away to her husband."

Comic lines (usually short) provide insight into
a character's personality and frequently highlight the
particularly impressive or ridiculous characteristic of
him or her. Late in *Losing Battles*, Miss Ora Stovall,
squeezed with others in the cab of the truck, perches on
Mrs. Moody's lap and identifies dwellings as they pass.
"'All right, that's Brother Bethune's house,' said Miss
Ora. 'He's a Baptist preacher and a moonshiner, and
that's his bluebird houses.'" The tone and the coordi-
nated elements in the sentence suggest that Miss Ora considers all three of Brother Bethune's roles of equal importance. His efforts at the reunion were, as we have

seen, marginal; but when he compares the long marriage of Grandpa (now dead) and Granny with the friendship of David and Jonathan, the ninety-year-old matriarch has had enough. "'Suppose you try taking a seat,' Granny was heard to say. 'Go over there in the corner.' She pointed to the old cedar log." When his prayers run too long, Granny knows what to do: "I'm putting a stop to that." And she does. Underlying this comic sequence is the tradition of the dominating woman quelling the timid and ineffective man with caustic words. Maud Eva Moody is another bossy woman. Dressed in Sunday white, wearing a wide-brimmed hat, and carrying a purse the size of a plum bucket, she can do little to rescue her Buick, but can give her husband orders. "You're fifty-five years old, had a warning about your blood pressure, suffer from dust and hay fever, and insisted on wearing your best seersucker today. You stay put—you hear me? You can give those boys directions." All this comes from a woman who attended Normal School for her teacher's training, majored in gym, and came forth to teach beginning physics because "that's what they were all starved for." Rosamond, the resourceful heroine in *The Robber Bridegroom*, meets dilemmas with common sense and, for the reader, with humor. Left with the choice of death or going home naked, Rosamond takes off for home. As Miss Welty wrote in *Fairy Tale of the Natchez Trace*, "The fairytale daughter, as we see, is also the child of her times, a straightforward little pioneer herself." Rosamond may have romantic illusions, but they do not subdue her common sense.

A character's manner of speaking often creates humor. The man from Connemara in "The Bride of Innisfallen" repeats "Oh, my God!" in response to everyone's statements. Having transformed Odysseus's men into swine and driven them outside using her wand as a broom, the beautiful and alluring Circe (in "Circe") speaks words more suited to a determined domestic than

to an immortal enchantress: "In the end it takes a phe-
nomenal neatness of housekeeping to put it through the
heads of men that they are swine." In "Shower of Gold,"
Katie Rainey meanders as she talks, from gossip to facts
to stories and secrets, and often gives her unidentified
listener a humorous appraisal of a hometown resident.
King MacLain, for instance, had "children of his growing up in the County Orphan's, so say several, and children known and unknown, scattered-like. When he does
come, he's just as nice as he can be to Snowdie. Just as
courteous. Was from the start."

The social and familiar aspects of comedy occur in
many of Miss Welty's occasional pieces. "The Flavor of
Jackson," the introduction to *The Jackson Cookbook* (1971),
begins with a reminder that Jackson citizens have tradi-
tionally dined at home. That custom was "our natural
form of hospitality" as well as "the most logical and eco-
nomical way to live." Important occasions could be cele-
brated at the Edwards House, but for many years Jackson was not heir to the famous restaurants synonymous
with the Gulf and New Orleans. The brief historical
discussion of social habits leads to a humorous climax. In
those earlier years in Jackson, "one Mexican at his hot-
tamale stand, on the corner of North West and Hamilton
during the cold months, couldn't make us cosmopolitan."
The "home-versus-city" pleasures occur again in a piece
called "The Little Store," included in *The Eye of the Story*.
A veritable delight for Jackson children, the little store in
the Welty neighborhood numbered among its entice-
ments a local drink called Lake's Celery. "What else
could it be called?" Miss Welty wrote. "It was made by a
Mr. Lake out of celery. It was a popular drink here for
years but was not known universally, as I found out
when I arrived in New York and ordered one in the
Astor bar."

When *Delta Wedding* appeared in 1946, several critics, including Diana Trilling, expressed their dis-

appointment. Mrs. Trilling regretted that this apparent
shift to the narcissistic southern fantasy drew Miss Welty
"away from the lower middle-class milieu of, say, The
[sic] Petrified Man."[5] That milieu, of course, was not
abandoned, but has been prominent in much Welty fiction since 1946, including *Losing Battles* and *The Optimist's
Daughter*. Within it, Miss Welty shows how well she
knows the southern poor—their faults, their deficiencies,
their virtues, their cadence of speech. Yet "she never
degrades or dehumanizes them by reducing them to a
stereotype."[6] The lower middle-class characters ring
true, from Leota ("Petrified Man," 1939) to Wanda
Fay Chisom McKelva (*The Optimist's Daughter*, 1972).
Although differences exist among these characters, they
nevertheless share many recognizable traits. Neither
Sister and her family, Mrs. Katie Rainey or her relatives the Mayhews, the Dalzells, the Chisoms, the
Beechams, the Renfros, Homer Champion, Ora Stovall,
or Pet Hanks assume privacy, and thus "life for them is a
matter of public display; they can only blunder forward
from moment to moment, unaware of any continuity to
experience."[7]

Lack of manners, sophistication, and experience
make these characters ready vehicles of humor. Eating
scenes, for example, amply illustrate their natural behavior. Over the hot kitchen stove, Sister tries "to stretch
two chickens over five people and a completely unexpected child into the bargain, without one moment's
notice." After Uncle Rondo has consumed enough of his
Fourth of July prescription to disport himself in Stella
Rondo's flesh-colored kimono, his stomach can only
tolerate cold biscuit and catsup. At Katie Rainey's funeral, her relatives appear from Stockstill and Lastingwell,
communities near the Tennessee line, having traveled in
pick-up trucks now drawn up to the porch. Along with
the adults "was a string of tow-headed children . . .
finishing some bananas," and they all came upon Virgie

at once, "kissed her in greedy turn and begged before they got through the door for ice water or iced tea or both." When court takes a noon recess in *The Ponder Heart*, the Peacock family perch on the courthouse stile to consume a meal Edna Earle can describe without seeing: "jelly sandwiches and sweet milk and biscuit and molasses in a tin bucket—poked wells in the biscuits to hold the molasses—and sweet potatoes wrapped in newspapers." They finish up with three or four watermelons "that couldn't have been any too ripe, to judge by what they left lying on the Courthouse grass for the world to see and pick up." The contents of the supper the Dalzells eat in the hospital waiting room are not named except for chicken legs, but since the meal was transported in shoe boxes and paper sacks, the reader, like Edna Earle, can make a pretty good guess at the entire menu. In the eyes of Mount Salus old timers, Judge McKelva succumbed to the unrefined ways of his new wife when he agreed to eat Sunday dinner in the Iona Hotel, at a table with no cloth, before a window that was unwashed.

Clothing images frequently add to the humor. While Laurel McKelva Hand "wore clothes of an interesting cut and texture" and donned her Sibyl Connolly suit for the return trip to Chicago, Wanda Fay delights in wearing long green ear drops and matching green shoes with stiletto heels; Bubba's windbreaker, Mrs. Chisom's tennis shoes, and Wendell's cowboy suit identify their taste in clothes. Leota urges Mrs. Fletcher to disguise her pregnancy by wearing a Stork-a-Lure dress, and Bonnie Dee Ponder was buried in "a Sunday-go-to-meeting dress, old-timey looking and too big for her—never washed or worn, just saved: white." Like clothing, keepsakes and possessions also indicate the unsophisticated taste of many characters. Sister treasures a picture of Nelson Eddy, bluebird wall vases, and an Add-a-Pearl necklace; Wanda Fay fancies peach-colored satin sheets. Ruby Fisher ("A Piece of News") considers a sack of

coffee marked in red letters "SAMPLE," sufficient payment for her afternoon with the traveling salesman. Bonnie Dee Peacock buys a washing machine and installs it
on the front porch. Reading material in Leota's beauty
shop includes a drugstore rental book, *Life Is Like That*,
and *Screen Secrets* magazine, and Mrs. Pike identifies Mr.
Petrie through a picture story in *Startling G-Man Tales*.
Furthermore, these characters' occupations seldom in-
volve professional training or extensive education: they
work in beauty shops, millinery shops, and country
stores; they farm, repair appliances, and operate wrecking concerns.

No self-consciousness overwhelms them; instead,
most are open and pleased with themselves, seldom examining their ways and means. For example, Homer
Champion sees his progress in life as a matter of pride. "I
grew up a poor Banner boy, penniless, ignorant, and
barefoot, and today I live in Foxtown in a brick veneer
home on a gravel road, got water in the kitchen, four
hundred chickens, and filling an office of public trust."
Homer's material status has improved to be sure, but he
has made little progress toward becoming more humane:
he has journeyed to Miss Julia's house on the very day
she died and told his story to get votes. Women characters often are vocal and domineering. Leota emasculates
her husband Fred, and Mrs. Fletcher relegates Mr.
Fletcher to a place of little significance. Other women are
not so distasteful, but all of them—Mrs. Chisom, Wanda
Fay, Mrs. Peacock, Beulah Renfro, Cleo Beecham, and
Maud Eva Moody—still manage and arrange and talk,
and leave their menfolk to take a back seat.

Wanda Fay Chisom is one of these lower middle-
class characters who attempt to leave that life behind,
and even denies that she has any family left alive. Physical details, however, link her irrevocably to her past. She
does not look forty "except [for] the lines of her neck and
the backs of her little square idle hands"; she is bony and

blue-veined, her eyes country blue, her face set with a little feisty jaw. Even in middle age, Fay gives the appearance of having been undernourished as a child. Her renunciation of her family is not permanent, and her attempt to move outside her class has not been successful. When her pregnant sister demands an excuse for Fay's returning to Texas with them to visit, Fay says, "I'd just like to see somebody that can talk my language, that's my excuse. . . . Where's DeWitt." Although Fay may prefer DeWitt's company now above all else, she has certainly been on home ground not only with the Chisoms who showed up at the funeral, but also with the Dalzells.

Generally, these lower middle-class characters lack intellectual curiosity, but they display close family loyalties and keep some continuity through these ties. Their behavior may not be exemplary, but the Dalzells crowd the hospital waiting room and they stick together. When the old lady disappears into the sickroom, she calls back that the others must not go off and leave her. The youngest of the Dalzell girls admits that their home, Fox Hill, may be harder to locate than Bigbee, but remoteness is compensated for by family. "But we don't think it's lonesome, because by the time you get all of us together, there's nine of us, not counting the tadpoles. Ten, if Granddad gets over this." Likewise, the Chisoms (except for Fay) have stayed close together, marriage increasing the nuclear family rather than splintering it. "Bubba pulled his trailer right up in my yard when he married and Irma can string her clothesline as far out as she pleases. Sis here got married and didn't even try to move away. Duffy just snuggled in." Their actions and words set them apart, but no pretense lurks long in their outlook or in their judgments of others. They will always remain baffled by a son's suicide or a daughter who chose to leave home, and committed to preserving the family. They judge others by the characteristics they themselves value. As Sis says to Laurel in parting, "We thought a heap of your old dad, even if he couldn't stay on earth long enough for us to get to know him. Whatever he was, we always knew he was just plain *folks.*"

Two relatively obscure Welty pieces are useful in looking at her comic work. "Hello and Good-Bye," which appeared in the July 1947 issue of *Atlantic,* lacks the biting satire of "Petrified Man," but combines actual experience (an assignment to photograph a pair of Mississippi beauty queens) with effective social satire. Set in Jackson on a hot summer afternoon, the story follows through a picture-taking sequence of a small-town, inexperienced beauty queen bound for New York City, her young chaperone-hostess, the sponsoring VFW representative, and the photographer. The young winner seems an unlikely selection. Utterly provincial, she says "Ma'am" to the photographer's questions, dresses inappropriately in black satin, clutches her patent leather purse in every picture, and trembles from homesickness and fright. The hostess is just as provincial, but considers herself worldly wise, having won the title "Miss Know-Your-Native-State-Better." She uses a Tallulah Bankhead voice when she can and considers herself a has-been because she gained nine pounds.

The photographer juxtaposes typical beauty contest glitter against backgrounds of political and military significance. The first picture poses queen and hostess in front of the Mississippi State Capitol and then in front of the cannon, on a little mound. (Here the hostess vaguely suspects something—"just sort of the idea . . . The *Cannon.*") The next background is a ship's figurehead, Columbia or some other patriotic lady. They return to the capitol and stand on the front steps, then on the top step, waving hello and good-bye, eyes fixed on the Robert E. Lee Hotel. At the photographer's suggestion, they strike the last poses in front of the Soldiers' Monument, which depicts a wounded soldier being aided by towering women identified as "our wives, our mothers, our daughters, our sisters." Even the VFW sponsor gets into these shots, after carefully adjusting his hat brim. They are a comic sight—the hostess smoothing her eyebrows with a wet finger and promising the VFW sponsor a long letter from New York City, and the shy, bewildered winner, fighting back tears and hunger and posing with her eyes rolled up, "like Little Eva dying."

The disparity between a frivolous beauty contest and important historical monuments draws no authorial comment. The narrative voice is the photographer's, who sees through the entire charade but photographs it without comment. By no means as successful as other early comic stories such as "Why I Live at the P.O." or "Lily Daw and the Three Ladies," "Hello and Good-Bye" does have a bittersweet humor. Told in retrospect, the story exposes the lack of elegance and sophistication, the near vulgarity of such useless displays of beauty. The dramatic new events in the life of the beauty queen bring her far more tears than joy, and the reader is led to sympathize with, rather than laugh at, her.

"Bye-Bye Brevoort," a Welty sketch written for *What Year Is This?*, bristles with comically absurd elements. The setting is a suite of rooms in New York's Brevoort Hotel on Fifth Avenue, occupied by Millicent Fortescue, Agatha Chrome, Violet Whichaway, and Miss Fortescue's maid Evans. The three old ladies are Brevoort relics, clinging to their dwelling, their antique silver service, and afternoon high teas, and oblivious to the fact that the Brevoort is being demolished. Their mutual friend Desmond Depree arrives for tea, and Evans, having been sent to get petit fours, enters the room on skates. Millicent, Violet, and Agatha all wear hearing aids; the ominous sounds of the wrecking crew go unnoticed, but the faint tinkle of the bell brings an instant response of "Tea Time!" Desmond shares their illusion. As the three building wreckers draw closer, one yells, "That's it. Hook a chain around the middle and drag her down." The reaction from the ladies is, "Did you speak, Desmond?" He did not, but thinks he can account for the noise: "I think that was someone in the corridor, dealing with a maid." As the wrecking noises continue, Millicent Fortescue thinks they come from the traffic and remarks that often she consoles herself "by pretending the traffic noises are simply pistol shots—the riff-raff *murdering* one another." The maid Evans knows all this is madness—"We're living in a Fool's Swiss Cheese"—but she turns from the dead telephone, picks up a seashell, and recites Longfellow: "It was the schooner Hesperus / That sailed the wintry sea." As the building wreckers beat on the door, Millicent instructs Evans to reply, "We are not at home." At last, the noisy alien force appears on the stage, only to be galvanized at the sight of the table shimmying. "Bye-Bye Brevoort" was part of the 1955 Revue at the Phoenix Theater, with Tammy Grimes as Violet Whichaway. The sketch was also presented in 1958 by the Jackson Little Theater.

Readers have their favorite comic pieces, but many would choose *The Ponder Heart* as Welty comedy at its sustained best. When the book appeared in 1954, one critic called it the most amusing piece of American humor since Mark Twain. Harrison Smith found it endowed with a magic sense of humor, and Charles Poore thought Miss Welty had never written a better story. In this superbly written monologue, Edna Earle relates facts and stories about Clay, Mississippi, and its residents, focusing her attention primarily on her Uncle Daniel, who has a loving heart and a low I.Q. Southern folk speech is brought to life "on every page in all of its color, vigor and raciness,"[8] and certainly in all of its humor, as numerous critics have noted in praising the skill, cleverness, and humor of Edna Earle's narration. Her cliches ("memory of an elephant," "pretty as a doll," "ignorance is bliss") may be numerous, but are never

tiresome. She can sum up a character succinctly. Judge
Clanahan's grandson DeYancey is "young and goes off
on tangents"; clipping coupons from *Movie Mirror* and
True Love Story occupies Bonnie Dee for hours while she
eats "the kind of fudge *anybody* could make." Informal
diction and colloquialisms vividly describe actions. Back
from their quick wedding in Silver City, Uncle Daniel
and Bonnie Dee "sashayed" into the Beulah Hotel; sometimes Bonnie Dee will "traipse"; and Narciss "will carry
Uncle Daniel home" (drive him in the Studebaker). Edna
Earle supplies Uncle Daniel with Fatimas to smoke by
"ordering off after them," and when life gets too complicated, "Judge Tip gets us out of fixes." Multiword modi-
fiers ("good-for-nothing canaries"), grammatical errors
("Bonnie Dee run me off"), characters' names (Intrepid
Elsie Fleming and Miss Teacake Magee), represent only
a sample of the rhetorical devices that add to the amusement.

   A primary comic device is the parody of important
events in Uncle Daniel's life—courtship, marriage, desertion, reconciliation, his wife's death and burial, and
his trial for murder. The courtship of seventeen-year-
old Bonnie Dee Peacock and Uncle Daniel bears no resemblance to the traditional ritual of a gentleman wooing
and winning a lady. Uncle Daniel entered Woolworth's
and announced "to the world in general and Bonnie Dee
at the jewelry counter in particular, 'I've got a great big
house standing empty and my father's Studebaker.
Come on—marry me.'" Their wedding lacked invita-
tions, rehearsal, and ceremony. With Narciss at the
wheel, they "went kiting off to Silver City, and a justice
of the peace with a sign in the yard married them."
Customary nuptial happiness was lessened because Bonnie Dee married on a trial basis and because the announcement of the wedding caused Uncle Daniel's father to
pop a blood vessel and die. (He was, as Uncle Daniel
reminded Edna Earle, always hard to please.) After five

years and six months, Bonnie Dee ended the trial marriage, and her desertion had serious effects. Dressed in a
sparkling white suit and shiny red tie, Uncle Daniel relates his sad tale to guests at the Beulah Hotel every
night, but at least Bonnie Dee's absence does not ruin his
appetite.

A reconciliation was not effected by Uncle Daniel
even though he knew Bonnie Dee had been seen in Memphis, a journey of only three hours and forty-five minutes by car. Edna Earle explains that Uncle Daniel
"wouldn't dream of going to Memphis to find Bonnie
Dee or Intrepid Elsie Fleming or you or anybody else.
Uncle Daniel belongs in Clay, and by now he's smart
enough to know it; and if he wasn't, I'd tell him." Judge
Tip Clanahan and Edna Earle placed a three-day ad in
the Memphis paper—a twelve-line poem in couplets—
and Bonnie Dee showed up the next morning at 9:45.'
Short-lived, the reconciliation failed when Bonnie Dee
threw Uncle Daniel out and occupied herself by ordering
dresses and appliances, installing electric power and a
telephone in the house, until he withheld her weekly
allowance, a step that brought messages to come home.
The reunion occurred during a violent afternoon thun-
derstorm which frightened Bonnie Dee so that Uncle
Daniel began tickling her with a tassel of an antimacas-
sar, beginning at her ankle and working up, sure that he
could calm her fear by playing "creep-mousie." Bonnie
Dee died laughing.

Her funeral was in Polk, not Clay, with the
Peacocks, not the Ponders, in charge; and every detail
lacked decorum and dignity. Two rawboned, red-headed
Baptist preachers presided in the little front room, where
the coffin was borne up by two kitchen chairs. Floral
arrangements were not of chrysanthemums, roses, or
gladiolas, but portulaca in pie pans, verbena growing in
an old auto tire, Jacob's-ladder tops and althea blooms
sewed on cardboard crosses, a salvia wreath with a bee in

it, and creek-bottom ferns that had drooped. Instead of
organ music and whispering, the noise of chickens was
heard beneath cracks in the floor, and the broom stood
sentinel behind the door. The bereaved husband got little attention, but he did get charged with murder.

In the trial (which occupies half of the book and
shows Miss Welty at her comic best), DeYancey Clanahan
argues Uncle Daniel's case, but does not want him to
testify. However, Uncle Daniel insists, and is thrilled to
be in the limelight. Before he makes too many incrimi-
nating statements, Edna Earle stops him, causing Uncle
Daniel to fling his arms on the witness stand, his coat
pockets bursting with money which he distributes
throughout the courtroom. Bedlam reigns as old Mrs.
Peacock hollers, "'Finders Keepers!'" and raises two
handfuls of money, and Dr. Ewbanks futilely demands,
"Stop him, Miss Edna Earle! Stop him, young lady!"
Almost lost in the commotion is the jury's verdict—"Not
guilty." Uncle Daniel, his money "all vamoosed," returns with Edna Earle to the hotel—nothing left but his
stories to tell again and again to whoever will sit and
listen.

Daniel Ponder's experiences as suitor, husband,
widower, and murder suspect sparkle with genial comedy, but neither he nor the other characters are exploited. Robert Giroux, an editor at Harcourt Brace in
1954, wrote Miss Welty his enthusiastic praise for Uncle
Daniel and Edna Earle, as well as for Narciss, Bonnie
Dee, Intrepid Elsie Fleming, and Miss Teacake Magee:
for him they were already immortal. A March 5, 1954,
letter from William Archibald reported that *The Ponder
Heart* moved him to immediate laughter and seemed a
legend and a classic already. Without doubt, *The Ponder
Heart* is "a parade of humorous characters in a pageant of
humorous episodes."[9]

From the ironic to the farcical, Eudora Welty's
humor enriches her work; overall, the humor is not rele-

gated to mere entertainment, but rather it is established as a staple of life and of fiction. Writing about "A Worn Path," Ruth M. Vande Kieft conjectured that Miss Welty attributed to Phoenix Jackson the three virtues of faith, hope, and love. To these virtues, Vande Kieft said, comedy is to be added. "Include a large measure of the comic spirit as part of hope, and you have the whole."[10] Seymour Gross's observation about *Losing Battles* applies to all Miss Welty's fiction that falls into the comic mode. "Comedy must make us feel, if for no longer than the enchanted time of reading, that Death and all those little deaths which are its harbingers have been triumphed over."[11]

Comedy sports with the frivolous, the ironic, and the satiric; it is quite able, Miss Welty has said, "to tackle the most serious matters that there are." When Charles Bunting quoted a *New York Times* critic who had written that "Eudora Welty possesses the surest comic sense of any American writer alive," Miss Welty's response made it clear that comedy is a sure foundation of her fiction. "I'm delighted that the critic thinks I have a good comic spirit. And I think that's taking me seriously."[12] It was Flannery O'Connor who reminded readers that her way of being serious was a *comic* one, and this is true also of Eudora Welty.

For the serious reader and critic of Eudora Welty's fiction, what comes from the comic spirit delights, to be sure, but it also informs. It should be no surprise that Faulkner's "library shelves held books that have a variety of places in histories of our humor—by Washington Irving, George Washington Harris, Mark Twain, Joel Chandler Harris, Bret Harte, James Branch Cabell, S. J. Perelman, Eudora Welty, and Nathanael West."[13]

3

~.'

Delight Ending
in Wisdom

To place Miss Welty's stories and novels into categories
or divisions calls for highly arbitrary decisions. Her work
shares many traits: a sense of the comic, arresting imagery, superb dialogue, a concern with human relationships and with the mystery of human life, and especially a thematic emphasis on mutability. Certainly, all
of her works give readers delight and wisdom; but, to a
degree, *A Curtain of Green*, *The Robber Bridegroom*, *The
Golden Apples*, and *Losing Battles* do so more directly
through dialogue, tale telling, and external confrontations than do *The Wide Net*, *Delta Wedding*, *The Bride of
Innisfallen*, and *The Optimist's Daughter*. In these last four
works, a sense of mystery often prevails, where internal
and reflective confrontations occur, where characters are
drawn into vortexes of quiet.

    A Curtain of Green and Other Stories (1941), Miss Wel-
ty's first book, appeared with two important preliminar-
ies: a dedication to her agent, Diarmuid Russell, and an
introduction by Katherine Anne Porter. Over the years,
some points in Porter's introduction have been challenged, but its presence then and now is a constant reminder that Miss Welty's career began with distinction.
As Porter noted, Miss Welty started writing "without
any particular encouragement, and, as it proved, not
needing any"; the stories at hand offered "an extraordinary range of mood, pace, tone, and variety of material."[1]

Jean Stafford did not find the stories consciously pro-
found, but saw in them an implicit astute commentary
on human behavior conveyed through humor; contrived
but clever architecture; arresting, if occasionally de-
formed, prose.[2] Some of the stories took on an almost
surrealistic note, but avoided escapism even when the
writing was detached from immediate controversial
subjects.[3] Critics drew comparisons to Kafka, Katherine
Mansfield, and Emily Dickinson, but were somewhat at
a loss in comfortably classifying the author of *A Curtain
of Green* as a southern or a regional writer.

If some of these stories resist systematic analysis,
they still convey deep feeling, at once delighting and
puzzling readers. The more thoughtful and sympathetic
Welty critics have found that what seems obscure, what
remains a puzzle, has been "a necessary means to the
embodiment of her great themes—the mystery and
changes of human personality and relationships."[4] Elizabeth Bowen divided writers into two categories: the
inventive and the creative. The inventive writer has a
plot, sufficiently lifelike characters, and a scene which
assumes a short-term reality. Such writers have a new
story to their credit, but their ideas come from the common stock. "No new world has been created, no unique
vision sheds light, nothing of significance has been laid
bare." Quite different is the creative writer whose work
"causes a long, reflective halt in the reader's faculties.
It demands to be reread, to be brooded over, to be in-
gested, to be lived with and *in*."[5] Eudora Welty, in all
of her work, Bowen declared, is a creative writer, whose
art invites contemplation and discovery.

The stories in *A Curtain of Green* must indeed be
lived with and in; they invite brooding and rereading.
The appearance of abnormal characters in many of them
prompted critics to call them grotesque and draw comparisons to Carson McCullers. Lily Daw ("Lily Daw and
the Three Ladies") may be so slow mentally that mar-

riage and being committed to the mental institution at Ellisville seem to her interchangeable choices, but she still triumphs over the three officious ladies bent on preserving appearances and propriety alone. Mr. Petrie's ("Petrified Man") claim of physically turning to stone is a counterpoint to the actions of Leota, Mrs. Pike, Thelma, and Mrs. Fletcher, who with their sharp tongues and wild-haired visages are latter-day Medusas housed in a lavender-colored beauty shop. Deaf and dumb, Ellie and Albert Morgan ("The Key") remain seated on the station bench as their long-awaited train roars by enroute to Niagara Falls, not knowing it has come and gone. Keela ("Keela, the Outcast Indian Maiden") turns out to be a little club-footed black man, not an outcast Indian maiden; but disguised or not, he has been a sideshow attraction, marveled at as he emitted weird sounds and devoured live chickens. Clytie, Octavia, and Gerald Farr ("Clytie") have grown so isolated in their father's house that they have lost touch with reality and exist in respective degrees of madness. Old Mr. Marblehall or Mr. Bird ("Old Mr. Marblehall") leads a double life maintaining two houses, two wives, and two sons, and obsessed with believing that the whole town "would die" if they knew his secret. Old Addie and her roommate ("A Visit of Charity"), trapped beyond the wavy hall floor and behind the heavy front door of the old folks' home, have become almost inhuman through the ravages of old age and senility. Sister and her entire family ("Why I Live at the P.O.") are eccentric and unloving, content to alienate one another and incapable of rationally solving their differences.

A *Curtain of Green* does have a liberal smattering of freaks, a type of character the southern writer can create, Flannery O'Connor said, because he can still recognize one. In Miss Welty's stories, these abnormal characters are, as one critic noted, absorbed, not exploited. For example, Mr. Petrie at age forty-two travels with the freak show and claims he can move his head only a quarter of an inch. His astonishing condition is fake, of course, but the complete insensitivity of the women in the story toward men in general, and their respective husbands in particular, is not. The presence of a supposed freak brings the real freaks—those who figuratively turn men to stone—to prominence. The two old women in "A Visit of Charity" are nearly dehumanized—they sound like sheep, their hands are quick as bird claws, they deny knowing each other even though they share the same room—but their irrational behavior in all its unpleasantness and pathos brings their visitor into focus. Marian is a Campfire Girl who visits the old folks' home to earn points, not to alleviate their loneliness. For added points, she will bring along a potted plant, but not the Bible; she has not embraced the altruistic goals of the Campfire Girls and she knows nothing of true charity. At the end, she retrieves her hidden apple and boards the rocketing bus, bound for the world of experience with no regret for lost innocence.

In at least six of the stories, dreams and fantasies overtake characters' total sense of reality. Home from her afternoon with the traveling coffee salesman, Ruby Fisher ("A Piece of News") spreads out the rain-soaked newspaper that had protected her payment of coffee and slowly spells out a piece of news: "Mrs. Ruby Fisher had the misfortune to be shot in the leg by her husband this week." Immediately identifying with the name, Ruby fantasizes melodramatically. If her husband Clyde did hear about the coffee salesman with the Pontiac car, would he shoot her? She imagines Clyde angry enough to shoot her in the heart, a wound miraculously not instantly fatal. Ruby would have a brand-new nightgown, her heart would hurt with every beat, her tears would show her extreme pain. Handsome, strong, and wild-haired, Clyde says unromantically and ungrammatically in her fantasy, "Ruby, I done this to you." The tragic

Ruby whispers with her dying breath, "That truth, Clyde—you done this to me." Ruby pla[ ]part aloud, "composing her face into a look which[ ]be beautiful, desirable, and dead." The fantasy continues. Clyde must buy her a new dress for the burial, dig a deep grave under the cedar tree, and nail up a pine coffin. All the while, "he would be wild, shouting, and all distracted, to think he would never touch her one more time." The constant rain is real and coincides with the tears she dreams Clyde sheds. Ruby's fantasy wound is more glamorous than a leg wound, and, amusing as it is, the imaginary episode reveals her longing for attention, her need to escape loneliness. She is not awakened by Prince Charming, but rudely brought to reality by the real Clyde poking her with the butt of his gun and growling, "'What's keeping supper?'" Not only is Ruby's temporary happiness gone, but Clyde laughs at her newspaper tale, since the actual shooting occurred in Tennessee to another Ruby Fisher. Suspicious of the unfamiliar newspaper, Clyde only "spanked her goodhumoredly across the backside." If he did know everything about the salesman, Clyde would not care enough to shoot Ruby in the leg or in the heart. She is left empty and lonely, her life as vague and dark as the night outside.

In "Powerhouse," a complicated story of separation, violence, and death set against a background of jazz improvisations, the protagonist Powerhouse is modeled on the great black jazz musician Fats Waller. Performing at a club, Powerhouse supposedly receives a four-word telegram saying "Your wife is dead." Did his wife, Gypsy, missing the traveling artist so much, really jump out of the window "and bust her brains all over the world"? The violence and death in Ruby Fisher's fantasy were pleasurable, bringing her the attention she longed for and never got in real life. In "Powerhouse," death and violence dominate a fantasy, but create only loneliness and grief. Powerhouse denies any reaction to the fictitious telegram saying: "What in the hell you talking about? Don't make no difference: I gotcha." The black musicians return from their intermission, and the dreadful telegram is left behind. Yet when one of the group asks Powerhouse if he intends to call Gypsy long distance as usual, he growls, "No!" The music starts, couples of different ages begin to dance, and the story ends with Powerhouse singing many choruses of a request song, "Somebody Loves You." The sentimental vocal search— "Somebody Loves You, I Wonder Who?"—emphasizes the uncertain state of Powerhouse and Gypsy; however, what Miss Welty had originally used at this point was a song Fats Waller recorded, "Hold Tight!" Editors at the *Atlantic Monthly*, which first published "Powerhouse," objected to the lyrics. "They wrote me that the *Atlantic Monthly cannot* publish those lyrics. I never knew why. I had to substitute 'Somebody Loves You, I Wonder Who' which is OK but 'Hold Tight' was marvelous. You know the lyrics with Fats Waller singing 'fooly racky sacky want some seafood, Mama!'"[6] *Atlantic*'s prudishness remains puzzling; compared to the romantic tune "Somebody Loves You," "Hold Tight!" is alive and sensual, a radically different song and perhaps a more honest and realistic message to Gypsy.

Less dramatic are the deaf and dumb couple in "The Key," Albert and Ellie Morgan of Yellow Leaf, Mississippi, who have lived their married life always saving for a trip to Niagara Falls. There, Albert fondly hopes, they might "even fall in love, the way other people have done." His wish is pure fantasy, for they will continue their sign-language quarrels and never find love. In "A Memory," a young girl once touches a friend's wrist, a moment he pretends not to notice, and the fantasy of her wished for and unrealized love begins. That love remains inviolable in fantasy, and when the young girl sees a family group cavorting on the beach, she is offended, her dream tarnished. The unreality of the girl's life contrasts sharply with the family of sea bathers, who are boisterous and vulgar in their antics, but who respond to each other, whose relationships are alive. The girl's artistic nature is not enough to balance her imagined view of love with life as it is actually lived. Even after many years have passed and she is no longer young, the episode does not seem trivial to her.

Four of the stories center on unexpected and shocking deaths which create bewilderment. In "The Hitch-hikers," Tom Harris, a thirty-year-old traveling salesman in office supplies, picks up two hitchhikers and stops overnight in Dulcie, where one hitchhiker, Sobby, hits the other one in the head with a bottle and kills him. The provocation for the murder (which happens in Harris's car) is senseless—"I was just tired of him always uppin' an' makin' a noise about ever'thing." The dead man, known only as Sanford, has no family, yet, ironically, he gains an identity in death. Harris the salesman is affable, generous, sought after, and yet he has no real identity, home, or ties. A part of the passing scene, he is at once free and helpless in a life where he always belongs temporarily:

there was often rain, there was often a party, and there had been other violence not of his doing—other fights, not quite so pointless, but fights in his car, fights, unheralded confessions, sudden love-making—none of any of that his, not his to keep, but belonging to the people of these towns he passed through, coming out of their rooted pasts and their mock rambles, coming out of their time.

R. J. Bowman, Miss Welty's other traveling salesman ("Death of a Traveling Salesman"), is, like Harris, in familiar territory, but he becomes completely disoriented. Seeking help, Bowman stumbles into the home of a country couple who are filled with pride, hope (an unborn baby), and love. His material world stands worthless in the face of their simple happiness. The fact of their noble actions "was suddenly too clear and too enormous within him for response." Bowman's destination is Beulah—a village in Bolivar County, Mississippi, as well as the destination of Bunyan's Pilgrim.[7] In Sonny and his woman, Bowman has glimpsed the human family, domestic and societal. Although he realizes that money and solitude are not enough, he remains alien to this domestic circle, and in a passage of unexpected lyric beauty, expresses the longings of a lonely man. "There would be a warm spring day.. . . . Come and stand in my heart, whoever you are and a whole river would cover your feet and rise higher and take your knees in whirlpools, and draw you down to itself, your whole body, your heart too." His realization is not enough, for he not only dies but dies alone, as he walks back to his car. "He covered his heart with both hands to keep anyone from hearing the noise it made. But nobody heard it."

"Flowers for Marjorie," the story of a young Mississippi couple caught in New York City during the Depression, ends disastrously, as Howard, despondent over finding no work and having no money or food, kills his pregnant wife with a butcher knife. The symbol of hope, the yellow pansy in the buttonhole of Marjorie's coat, and the relentless symbol of time, the old alarm clock that Howard smashes, indicate the irreconcilable forces of Marjorie's persistent optimism and Howard's chronic despair. Ironically, once the murder is done, Howard goes out and encounters a series of fortunate events which relieve his financial plight. Like Howard, Mrs. Larkin ("A Curtain of Green") is driven to commit a senseless act of violence, but she, at the last moment, is brought back, released from her despair. From her front porch, Mrs. Larkin has seen her husband drive in from work and, before he can get out of the car, be crushed to death when an enormous, fragrant chinaberry tree falls. His sudden death drives her from reality; her days are now spent haphazardly planting in her garden, which reminds her neighbors of a jungle. Coming upon her black helper Jamey kneeling at his work, Mrs. Larkin approaches, hoe in hand, about to strike another senseless blow of death—"so helpless was she, too helpless to defy the workings of accident, of life, of death, of unaccountability." The rain which daily falls at Larkin's Hill comes at this moment, releasing Mrs. Larkin from her violent temptation. "Then as if it had swelled and broken over a daily levee, tenderness tore and spun through her sagging body."

Included in *A Curtain of Green* are many of Miss Welty's most frequently anthologized stories. The last story in the collection, "A Worn Path," embodies the quintessence of selfless devotion and human endurance. Old Phoenix makes her arduous journey for the grandson's medicine, enduring trials and humiliations along her way, but faithfully continuing because the task must be done. The collection remains impressive in every aspect and a source of pride, as John Woodburn said upon its publication.

Perhaps the most noteworthy reaction to *The Robber Bridegroom* was also the shortest—a two-line letter from William Faulkner (in Hollywood), "on a little piece of notebook paper, written in that fine, neat, sort of unreadable hand, and in pencil—and I've lost it."[8] The lost message had succinctly stated that Faulkner liked the little book called *The Robber Bridegroom.* Although reviewers in 1942 were not unanimous in their praise, *The Robber Bridegroom* received considerable notice. Later critics think that this significant work has been somewhat neglected; certainly, interpretations of it have differed widely. The starting point now should be Miss Welty's own commentary, her published paper *Fairy Tale of the Natchez Trace*, delivered to the Mississippi Historical Society in 1975. What she had *not* done, Miss Welty told the group, was write a *historical* historical novel; instead, she had taken historical liberties on occasion and by design had made local history, legend, and Grimms' fairy tales into working equivalents in the story. All three sources, she pointed out, supplied ample detail. The short novel did not bury itself "deep in historical fact," she declared, but "flew up, like a cuckoo, and alighted in the borrowed nest of fantasy."

The Robber Bridegroom is a book whose essential criterion is tone. When local legend emerges from the Natchez Trace, fearsome deeds attend it, a fact Elizabeth Bowen noted in writing of her trip through that territory. "When there have been robbers, there are robbers always. Folklore makes a terrain of its own, full of fears, agonized acts of daring, captures, obliterated graves, unexpunged bloodstains, ever-lurking vengeances."[9] The unsavory qualities of Little Harp and what remains of Big Harp are as familiar as they are fearsome—they come out of that legend, recognized as such and relegated to horrors of the past. Fairy tales, too, combine the horrible and the beautiful, as (again) Elizabeth Bowen pointed out in noting the centenary of the Brothers Grimm. Such tales may be monstrous, irrational, and unnatural, but "few dooms in this perilous world are permanent, it is consoling to remember . . . this world of the tales is a blend of coziness and bloodthirstiness, of slapstick comedy, coarse-grained good sense and inadvertent, ethereal beauty."[10]

Bloodthirsty acts do happen in *The Robber Bridegroom*: Mike Fink thinks he beat Clement Musgrove and Jamie Lockhart to death as they slept in the same bed at the inn; deep in Clement's past is the Indian massacre where his infant son was plunged in boiling oil, his wife dying at the sight, and Kentucky Thomas was killed, leaving his wicked and ugly wife Salome to later marry Clement; Little Harp does rape and murder the Indian girl; the group of robbers are done away with by the Indians; and Salome, having defied the sun, is doomed to dance herself to death. All these events, however, are balanced by the light-hearted tone. *The Robber Bridegroom*, Miss Welty concluded in her remarks to the historians, was "an awakening to a dear native land and its own story of early life, made and offered by a novelist's imagination in exuberance and joy."

That exuberance and joy come from the crucial theme of doubleness expressed in Clement Musgrove's frequently cited words ("For all things are double, and this should keep us from taking liberties with the outside world, and acting too quickly to finish things off) and in the realization of Rosamond (his beautiful daughter) that "the heart cannot live without something to sorrow and be curious over." Single vision is hopelessly inadequate. One must accept the paradoxes—the ugly side of the beautiful, the dishonest face of the honest—and still live. The exuberance and joy also come from the numerous richly comic scenes, many of them slapstick. Goat, the doltish neighbor of Clement Musgrove and clown counterpart of the handsome robber bridegroom Jamie Lockhart, is hired by the jealous Salome to follow and harm Rosamond. Deterred by Jamie's talking raven, who says, *"Turn back, my bonny, / Turn away home,"* Goat, "who never disobeyed any orders as plain as that, had turned at once and gone back to his mother." Returning penniless again, Goat receives his mother's angry wish that she had strangled him at birth, the selfsame wish Salome utters when Goat reports his failure with Rosamond. Goat remarks that Salome now makes two that think he should have been strangled at birth, but comforts himself that the number is small. Trying to speak to Big Harp's severed head (which is kept in the trunk and repeatedly commands, "Let me out!"), Goat responds, "'What did you say?' . . . bending down to put his ear to the top. 'Repeat it, please, for I am a little hard of hearing when there is a conversation through a trunk.'"

Juxtapositions, paradoxes, and imagery create other

humorous episodes. Clement Musgrove knows he will
have bedfellows on a stormy night at the inn (such being
the custom), and three to a bed notwithstanding, he
obeys the rule of the house by taking off his boots before
retiring. Unsuccessful in stopping his lovely daughter's
lies (which come like pearls), Clement threatens her with
the Female Academy or with tutoring in the unlikely
combination of Greek, sewing, and guitar. Rosamond
takes tender and equal care of *each* treasure her robber
bridegroom brings her, although "she did not know
when she could ever find use for a thousand pieces of
English silver or the scalp of a Creek." Chancing upon
the robbers' den, Rosamond immediately sets it straight,
shoveling ashes, scrubbing the hearth, carrying in wood,
laying a new fire, putting the kettle on to boil. Her
efforts, however, are not met with gratitude, but with
consternation. "What bastard has been robbing the
place?" Once settled into this strange household, Rosamond does her best to domesticate the robbers and
attend to their needs. Before they leave on their daily
ravages, "she packed them lunches to take with them in
the mornings, a bucket for each, in case they became
separated before they would have their food at noon over
the fire of an oak tree. And she wove a mat of canes and
rushes and made them wipe their feet when they came in
at the door." Robbers and murderers they may be, but
they are well fed and clean shod. Clement battles a wil-
low tree all night; the priest Father O'Connell is the
whiskey supplier; Salome dresses finely when Jamie
Lockhart comes to dinner, but her jewels "gave out
spangles the way a porcupine gives out quills" and from
the dining table she calls at the top of her lungs to Rosamond in the kitchen. Even Salome's death is funny.
Forced to dance because she defied the sun, Salome
whirls faster and faster, casting petticoats "until at the
end she danced as naked as a plucked goose." Blue as a
thistle, she fell down stone dead; her body "was tied to a

bony pony, and Clement was given the rope to lead it away." The rhyme "bony pony" makes it difficult to grieve long for Salome.

Humor surrounds the legendary Mike Fink. At the beginning of the novel, he demands that his listeners recognize his identity and acknowledge him as the doer of these extraordinary deeds. Near the end of the novel, however, he is an ordinary mail rider and now is anxious that his real identity be kept secret. The reputation of Mike Fink does not easily fit the image of a mail rider.

If *The Robber Bridegroom* is, as some have said, "an examination of the theme of disenchantment in the pursuit of a pastoral, and fundamentally American, Eden,"[11] it is equally true that its deadpan jokes are still funny over thirty years later.[12] Alfred Kazin's review appeared in the *New York Herald Tribune Book Review* on October 25, 1942, and his comments revealed the heart of the book. Miss Welty captured what others had been unable to because she was not writing history but was "writing out of a joy in the world she has restored, and with an eye toward the comedy and poetry embedded in it. . . . What composes the book is a series of fairy-tale incidents dense beyond retelling, the traditional comedy of errors perched crazily on wickedness and innocence."[13] Mingling ancient fairy tales with legends of the Natchez Trace, *The Robber Bridegroom* amuses and delights and mildly terrorizes; but on the whole, it does not engage the reader's emotions as do works like *The Golden Apples* and *Losing Battles*.

The Golden Apples (1949), one of Miss Welty's most impressive books, is the work she describes as in a way "closest to my heart of all my books." Her pleasure encompasses the whole book: "Harcourt only issues it now as a paperback. . . . And it was a beautiful hard-cover edition, just a lovely book; I mean, the job of book making. It had a beautiful jacket. Everything about it I liked."[14] Made up of seven interrelated stories, *The Golden*

Apples had never been assigned to a genre that satisfied all critics. About halfway through, Miss Welty said she realized the stories were connected. Characters come from families in Morgana, Mississippi, or nearby Mac-Lain, and forty years pass between the opening mono-logue of Katie Rainey ("Shower of Gold") and the last story ("The Wanderers"), which centers around her funeral. A list of the eight main families of Morgana and of seven lesser ones appears, along with eight black char-acters' names. Some critics insist that *The Golden Apples* is best read as a novel, albeit a loosely knit one. Although Miss Welty agrees that additional meaning may come when the stories are read as a group, she has adamantly maintained that they do not constitute a novel. Furth-ermore, *The Collected Stories of Eudora Welty*, published in the fall of 1980, includes *The Golden Apples* and that inclu-sion is perhaps her final word on the subject. Thomas L. McHaney suggests that these stories do at least form a cycle, as songs or myths may, and this is a helpful view even if it does not settle the genre question altogether.

A host of human adventures transpires during the forty-year span—wanderers leave and at last return to stay as others prepare to depart, vigorous people grow old and relinquish their realm of authority, some people marry and produce children, still others go mad, die in old age, or commit suicide. When *The Golden Apples* appeared, reviewers were at odds over the most and the least successful stories, some extravagantly praising the ones others found weak. Suffice it to say, *The Golden Apples* is one of Miss Welty's most rewarding and de-manding books.

The aspect of the work that has received the most critical attention is the use of myth, the studies often as exhausting as they are exhaustive. The paradoxical good and evil associations with the golden apples of myth and the exploits of Perseus are clearly in evidence. Almost every critic has pointed out the counterparts of King

MacLain as Zeus, Morgana-style, and Snowdie his
wife as Danäe. (Snowdie returns impregnated from her
meeting in the woods with King, looking, Katie Rainey
reports, "like a shower of something had struck her, like
she'd been caught out in something bright.") In "Sir Rabbit," Mattie Will Sojourner Holifield plays Leda to King
MacLain's swan while Eugene and the Spanish guitarist
("Music from Spain") recall deeds of Hercules, Antaeus,
and Ulysses. In a 1973 study, Thomas L. McHaney
argues that myth operates here on two levels. Characters
may be surrounded by myth in a natural way, but "part
of Miss Welty's allusion is also surely intentional, a de-
liberate effort to display one or two prime myths within.
the general mythological context in order to underscore
the principal concerns of the book."[15]

Since lines from Yeats's poem "Song of the Wandering Aengus" are quoted in "June Recital," readers cannot
ignore Miss Welty's sources. She herself knows existing
folklore and has used "not only Mississippi folklore but
Greek and Roman myths or anything else, Irish stories,
anything else that happens to come in handy that I think
is an expression of something that I see around me in
life."[16] What is there to be plucked, she adds, should be.
As fascinating and complex as the trails are in these stories that link ancient myth to characters' lives in Morgana,
Miss Welty's own extraordinary creativity must not be
slighted: she has created a town and populated it with
families whose fortunes are fascinating and enduring.

Miss Welty explained that her own postage-stamp
world of Morgana, Mississippi, is

a made-up Delta town. I was drawn to the name because I
always loved the conception of *Fata Morgana*—the illusory
shape, the mirage that comes over the sea. All Delta places have
names after people, so it was suitable to call it Morgana after
some Morgans. My population might not have known there
was such a thing as *Fata Morgana*, but illusions weren't unknown to them, all the same—coming in over the cottonfields.[17]

Reviewers and critics picked up the *Fata Morgana* associations even before Miss Welty herself had commented
on it; William M. Jones, for example, made connections
with the first canto of Walter Scott's *Marmion*, when the
Champion of the Lake enters Morgana's fated house. As
meaningful as these observations are, the fact remains
that in original publications of the individual stories and
throughout the typescript of the collection, the name of
the town where the Morrisons and the Raineys, the Mac-
Lains and the Carmichaels, the Spights and the Moodys,
the Loomises and the Holifields, live is "Battle Hill."[18] At
some stage before *The Golden Apples* was published, "Battle Hill" was replaced with "Morgana." Other name
changes also occurred. "June Recital" was first published
as "Golden Apples," and "The Wanderers" as "The
Hummingbirds." Mattie Will Oliver became Mattie Will
Sojourner (a surname used in *Losing Battles*); Nina Forrest
became Nina Carmichael; Mr. Hi Watkins, Mr. Holifield; the Howard family, the Morrison family; and
Nola, Twosie.

The stories differ greatly in length—"Shower of
Gold" and "Sir Rabbit" are decidedly shorter than the
other five, and "June Recital" is by far the longest of the
seven. Many of the same characters weave in and out of
these stories, and if any one theme dominates, it is that of
the loneliness which overtakes most of the characters'
lives to some degree. For example, Katie Rainey in
"Shower of Gold" has friends, her husband Fate, and her
children Virgie and Victor, and hints she may have enjoyed the favors of King MacLain. But by the end of the
monologue, her friend Snowdie MacLain has become
estranged from her, and by the time the reader meets
Katie in "The Wanderers," she is old and crippled from a
stroke, unable even to milk her cows. She has lost her
husband; her son Victor was killed in World War I (she
threw herself on his coffin, returned from France), and
she now has only Virgie, who has gone away once and

who leaves again the day after Katie is buried. An especially lonely character, Snowdie Hudson MacLain cares
for her unruly twins, Randall and Eugene, and waits for
her absent husband King, who is gone by turns a week or
years. Her sons both make unhappy marriages. In the
end, having spent her parents' money on detective fees,
Snowdie at last has King home to stay, but now, as she
murmurs to Virgie Rainey, "I don't know what to do
with him."

All of the Morrisons are lonely. Wilbur, the father,
is overruled by his wife and exists in his life as editor of
the *Bugle*. Catherine has no more success with her children than she does with her husband, and at last kills
herself. Malaria temporarily isolates her son Loch, but
when he is grown, he leaves Morgana for New York City
and continues his isolation, maintaining a connection
with his hometown only by an occasional letter. Cassie
Morrison, shut up in her room tie-dyeing a scarf, is the
character blessed with remembering Yeats's "Song of the
Wandering Aengus," but she does not follow the quest,
she makes no search for the golden apples. In the end,
she is a dull and boring spinster at Katie Rainey's funeral, her true nature full of platitudes and her personality
epitomized by small actions: "Cassie had chosen the one
thin, gold-rimmed coffee cup for herself and balanced it
serenely." Her contact with real life remains unexplored;
she is just what she was at the end of the hayride when
she was sixteen and had "let nobody touch even her
hand." Loneliness claims Miss Eckhart, the German
piano teacher, whose love for Mr. Sissum remains unre-
quited and whose devotion to Virgie Rainey goes unre-
warded. Bereft of pupils, piano, and living quarters, she
ends up a ward of the county. Loneliness overwhelms
both Eugene and Randall MacLain, and certainly Virgie
Rainey, who, in spite of Miss Eckart's encouragement
and praise, did not go away and become a famous musician, and in spite of numerous love affairs, is still single,

left at the end of the book with only a nameless, old, wrapped-up black woman with a red hen under her arm.

MacLain family members appear in one way or another in all seven of the stories. Katie Rainey tells the nameless passerby in "Shower of Gold" the story of Snowdie and King MacLain and their twins. In "June Recital," Snowdie is Miss Eckhart's landlady and greets parents at the front door on recital night. Eugene, the only boy pupil, gets free piano lessons and opens every recital with the same piece, "The Stubborn Rocking Horse." In "Sir Rabbit," Eugene and Randall (now fifteen) will, as their father does in this story, enjoy the wood nymph creature Mattie Will. Ran MacLain appears briefly in "Moon Lake," which centers on the weeks at camp for the county orphans and the town children and somewhat on Loch Morrison, the camp life guard. Jinny Love assures Etoile that "Anybody knows him, and his twin brother too." "The Whole World Knows" relates Ran MacLain's marital difficulties with Jinny Love Stark, his shabby affair with Maideen Sumrall (who commits suicide), and his pleas to the ever-absent King, "Father, I wish I could talk to you, wherever you are right now." Eugene's story, "Music from Spain," takes place in San Francisco, where, as a watch repairman at Bertsinger's Jewelry, he lives with his wife and former landlady, Emma. His great sorrow, the death of his young daughter Fan, remains unassuaged, and his mysterious day-long adventure with the non–English-speaking Spanish guitarist does not resolve his difficulties. His slapping Emma that morning signals a break in character, but by evening and his return home, she has forgotten and remarks characteristically, "You've left your hat somewhere. . . . I'll be burying you next from pneumonia." King MacLain, the legendary wanderer, now in his sixties and returned home for good, lurks around Katie Rainey's funeral in "The Wanderers," making faces at Virgie, eating at the buffet, and knowing

what they all know—that he will be the next to die. At
Katie's burial, all pass Eugene's grave (his wife did not
come to the funeral) and all see Randall, middle-aged and
reunited with Jinny Love and their children. He smiles
and shakes hands all around; he had been elected mayor
"for his glamour and his story, for being a MacLain and
the bad twin, for marrying a Stark and then for ruining a
girl and the thing she did."

Für Elise—Beethoven

Miss Welty's musical interest has never been better
employed than in "June Recital," where Beethoven's delicate piano melody *Für Elise* symbolizes the past and
embodies the passionate feeling that music evokes in
those who respond to it. To while away his convalescent
hours, Loch Morrison peers through his father's tele-
scope, minutely surveying the vacant house next door
where Snowdie MacLain used to live. Music enters the
story with Loch's factual observation: "There was a
piano in the parlor." Virgie Rainey and her sailor, "Kew-
pie" Moffit, slip in through the back door, their usual
path, and, before Loch watches their bedroom romp, he
hears the opening notes of *Für Elise* ("A little tune was
playing on the air, and it was coming from the piano in
the vacant house"). Loch's behavior thus far in the story
has been typical of a young boy frustrated over being
housebound in June with chills and fever. Each time his
mother comes to him bearing a spoonful of cocoa-
quinine, he yells until his breath gives out and then swal-
lows. He unsuccessfully tries to persuade Louella, the
black cook, to get him an ice cream cone at Loomis's

drugstore with her own money. When Cassie leaves his room, he yells after her that she looks silly, and when his mother brings some junket, "he made a noise calculated to sicken her." His reaction to the music, however, reveals an altogether different nature. The notes of *Für Elise* (played at this moment by Virgie Rainey) come to him "like a touch from a small hand . . . like a signal, a greeting—the kind of thing a horn would play out in the woods." Loch's mouth falls open in astonishment and tears come into his eyes as the melody seems the only thing accountable in his whole life. It transports him from the present into a time long ago when his sister was so sweet, when she and Loch had loved "each other in a different world, a boundless, trustful country of its own where no mother or father came, either through sweetness or impatience." That country of pleasant memory stands opposite Loch's present, solitary world "where he looked out all eyes like Argus, on guard everywhere."

A third visitor to the vacant house comes up the walk, old and disheveled, and Loch watches her with a sense of *déjà vu* as she laboriously begins her mock decoration of the parlor with newspapers. Symbolically, Miss Eckhart (the old woman) pushes a statue out of the way and sets a brown wooden box shaped like an obelisk in its place on the piano, then sticks out one finger and plays the melody. The statue is dear to Miss Eckhart: when she gave piano lessons in this very recital room, "on the right-hand corner of the piano stood a small, mint-white bust of Beethoven, all softened around the edges with the nose smoothed down, as if a cow had licked it." Now the bust of Beethoven is replaced by the mechanical metronome, and Miss Eckhart's own piano playing is reduced to holding out one finger to play the great melody. The power and passion of former days are gone.

When the notes of *Für Elise* sound for the third time, Cassie Morrison instinctively responds with "Virgie

Rainey, *danke schoen*," since *Für Elise* had always been *her* piece. Unable to believe Virgie is in the vacant house and producing the music, Cassie doubts that she even heard it; then, as if to verify its existence, the notes come again. "This time there were two phrases, the *E* in the second phrase very flat." At this moment, the melody and lines from Yeats's poem bring the past to Cassie in a flood, and the plot retreats into the past for the story of Miss Eckhart and her pupils.

Lotte Elisabeth Eckhart and her old mother are outsiders. Why they came to Morgana no one knows and nothing of their past secrets is revealed. A few German words—*danke schoen, Kuchen, mein liebes kind*—Miss Eckhart's old-fashioned dress, her cooking cabbage the way nobody else does, her front-door wine deliveries by Dago Joe, and her unchallenged authority at recital time, set her apart and mark her lonely life. Cassie remembers the piano lessons. A mistake brought a slap from the fly-swatter; a perfect performance brought no praise (except for Virgie), just the words "Enough from *you* today," as Miss Eckhart tapped the bars of her canary's cage. Whatever dreams and ambitions she had are now fixed on Virgie, who brashly defies the teacher, refusing the discipline of the metronome and playing a rondo her way. When a new sheet of music keeps rolling back up, Virgie throws it on the floor and jumps on it, an act Cassie considers heartless. Virgie's willful caprices finally affect Miss Eckhart so that Cassie sees her spirit diminish and become like "a terrifyingly gentle water-buffalo cow in the story of 'Peasie and Beansie' in the reader. And sooner or later, after taming her teacher, Virgie was going to mistreat her. Most of them expected some great scene." The scene did come.

In spite of her lonely surroundings and, except for Virgie, her mediocre pupils, Miss Eckhart reveals her passionate response to music on a summer afternoon when Virgie, Cassie, and Jinny Love Stark are caught in

her studio by a sudden storm. With no warning, Miss
Eckhart began to play "as if it were Beethoven." She
herself is transformed, her face sightless, one for music
only: "the face a mountain could have, or what might be
seen behind the veil of a waterfall. . . . And if the sonata
had an origin in a place on earth, it was the place where
Virgie, even, had never been and was not likely even to
go." Except for the recital quartets, Miss Eckhart has
never played for any pupils; when she dropped her hands
that afternoon, the three girls "all cried in startled recoil"
for her to play again. Her response, a simple "NO." The
music Miss Eckhart played was difficult and when she
made mistakes, she went back and played the passage
correctly. When Jinny Love, who had carefully turned
the pages as Miss Eckhart played, stepped forward and
closed the music, the girls "saw it wasn't the right music
at all for it was some bound-together songs of Hugo
Wolf." Snowdie MacLain asks Miss Eckhart what she
had played, and the answer is merely, "I couldn't say . . .
I have forgotten." Her youth, talent, and passion revived
during the time of the playing, but now are gone, as is
the title of the music.

The musical allusions here are complicated and remain a bit puzzling. First, we do not learn what Miss
Eckhart actually played so unexpectedly and so relentlessly, nor do we know why the summer storm prompted the performance. Her German origin and the bust of
Beethoven suggest that she may have played one of that
composer's sonatas, but the narrative voice has said she
played "as if it were Beethoven," not declaring that it
was. Further, the bound-together songs of Hugo Wolf
provide insight into Miss Eckhart's (and Miss Welty's)
musical knowledge. Philip L. Miller, in *The Ring of
Words*, considers Hugo Wolf (1860–1901) the acknowledged master among lieder composers. Totally absorbed
in poetry, Wolf concentrated on one poet until he ex-
hausted the material he could set to music. Only recent-

ly, Miller says, "have the songs of Wolf begun to be
generally known, for with a few exceptions they were too
difficult for the once flourishing amateur singer and pian-
ist, nor have many of them been considered 'grateful'
enough for the recital singer."[19] Miss Eckhart begins
teaching piano in Morgana before 1918 (her pupil list
dwindles after the war starts and anti-German sentiment
emerges) and by then her copy of the Wolf songs "was in
soft yellow tatters." Both Miss Eckhart and her creator,
Eudora Welty, admired Wolf long before it was com-
monplace to do so outside of Germany. Even in 1947, the
original publication date of "June Recital," the phono-
graph record had not yet built a wide audience for the
lieder of Hugo Wolf.

Each June the recital was elaborate, replete with
secret preparations for new dresses, colored sashes,
printed programs, and parlor decorations; and parents
were packed in tight with no electric fans permitted until
after the music. Performances and flower presentations
followed a regular pattern, and all the pupils, except
Virgie, played their worst. The program always began
with "The Stubborn Rocking Horse" and ended with
"Marche Militaire" for eight hands. For this last recital,
Cassie struggles through *Rustle of Spring* and Virgie plays
quite well the *Fantasia on Beethoven's Ruins of Athens*, displaying a streak of red around her sash as she finishes.
Virgie, however, never gets close to the concert stage,
and her performance fades, forgotten as she snaps on
her piano light at the Bijou Theater. Now joined to the
world of Gish, the Talmadge sisters, and Valentino, Virgie accompanies the pictures on the silent screen with
renditions of "You've Got To See Mama Every Night,"
"Avalon," "Kamennoi-Ostrow," or "Anitra's Dance."
The symbolic link between Virgie and Miss Eckhart, the
Beethoven melody *Für Elise*, is now something Virgie
plays in snatches and, ironically, only during advertise-
ments. The June recital whose end signaled the begin-

ning of vacation had found Virgie Rainey playing harder and harder pieces better and better, but ultimately Miss Eckhart's world of Beethoven and Liszt and Hugo Wolf is abandoned for the Bijou and "You've Got To See Mama Every Night."

The climax of "June Recital" comes when Miss Eckhart and Virgie, both now ejected from the smoking house (Miss Eckhart had set fire to the newspaper decorations), meet on the dead-quiet sidewalk and pass with no word of greeting, reproach, or regret. They were both, the narrative voice says, "human beings terribly at large, roaming on the face of the earth . . . like lost beasts." The ties associated with Virgie and music appear again in the last story, "The Wanderers," where she at last makes her peace with Miss Eckhart, now long dead. In the cemetery Virgie is able to see where Miss Eckhart is buried: "There was the dark, squat stone Virgie had looked for yesterday, confusing her dead." Miss Eckhart's roaming on the face of the earth is done, whatever ambitions she hoped to realize through Virgie Rainey, dead for some twenty-five years. Oddly enough, Virgie's musical compromise comes back to her late on the night her mother is buried, when an old country woman pounds on the door bringing a night-blooming cereus, telling her to look at the flower now since tomorrow it will be like a wrung chicken's neck. Departing, the woman speaks of Virgie's days at the Bijou. "'You used to play the pi-anna in the picture show when you's little and I's young and in town, dear love,' she called, turning away through the dark. 'Sorry about your Mama; didn't suppose anybody make as pretty music as you *ever* have no trouble—I thought you's the prettiest little thing ever was.'"

Much of the burden of life that the characters in *The Golden Apples* have undergone is defined in "The Wanderers" by the painting Virgie Rainey remembers hanging

over the dictionary in Miss Eckhart's studio. "It showed
Perseus with the head of the Medusa. 'The same thing as
Siegfried and the Dragon,' Miss Eckhart said, as if explaining second best." The underlying paradox in the
encounters of Perseus with Medusa and Siegfried with
the Dragon (Fafner, the giant transformed to better
guard the stolen gold), is that the heroic act requires a
victim. Heroism is not a simple matter of good triumphant over evil.[20] Miss Eckhart had understood the picture, had hung it on the wall herself. "She had absorbed
the hero and the victim and then, stoutly, could sit down
to the piano with all Beethoven ahead of her." Knowing
full well that Virgie might desert her gift, Miss Eckhart
still offered her *the* Beethoven, which Virgie, in the
strange wisdom of youth accepted, "as with the dragon's
blood." Now as Virgie leaves Morgana, the dead, and
the past, a melody (*Für Elise*) softly lifts of itself and at
every beat of the notes the hero claims his victim; good
and evil, truth and betrayal, love and death are bound
together—"Endless the Medusa, and Perseus endless."

The richness of *The Golden Apples* eludes and defies
any final word. Engaging themes of loneliness and
separation, the unsuccessful search for love, the urge to
wander, the mystery of human life, the disparity between expectation and fulfillment, course their way
through the seven stories, making characters and readers
confront significant issues of life. Characters are distinct
in dress, speech, behavior, and ambitions; they exist in
the fascinating web of small southern-town life where all
the townspeople know everything about each other—or
at least think they do. In Randall and Jinny Love Mac-
Lain's children, *The Golden Apples* touches the third generation, and knowledge of every family in Morgana ex-
tends forward and backward unless an outsider blocks
access to it, as Miss Eckhart does. Miss Welty's eternal
good humor threads its way through the stories, her

matchless gift for simile and detail shown here is sur-
passed only in *Losing Battles*, and her unerring ear pro-
duces the believable speech of Morgana's populace.

Some scenes are Joycean epiphanies—Miss Eckhart's piano performance during the summer storm,
Loch Morrison's introspection after reviving the nearly
drowned Easter, Eugene's return home after the adven-
turous day with the Spanish guitarist, and particularly
Virgie Rainey's nude swim, where "she hung suspended
in the Big Black River as she would know to hang suspended in felicity." The critical attention *The Golden Apples* continues to receive attests to its complex richness
and to its enduring qualities. Merrill M. Skaggs spoke for
many readers when he called *The Golden Apples* "unparal-
leled and unapproached. We simply take off our hats
and let Miss Welty go first."[21]

When *Losing Battles* was published in 1970, it repre-
sented the beginning of a third act in Miss Welty's writing career, a phase entered into with zest and skill. By far
the longest of her novels, *Losing Battles* covers a day and a
half in clock time, but weaves in details of Renfros and
Beechams for four generations, along with tales of their
various neighbors. As Louise Gossett suggests, it is a
novel of festival and celebration—Granny Vaughn's
ninetieth birthday rallies a day-long family reunion
which brings kith and kin from their respective homes,
and Jack, the fair-haired great-grandson, from the prison
in Parchman, to be in attendance. Stylistically, *Losing
Battles* is externalized, the major portion carried through
dialogue, with the narrative voice given little space to
comment, analyze, or judge. Talk is in unending variety.
As Robert Heilman explains:

We are plunged into tall tales, folk humor, slapstick episodes of
unruly persons and objects, all these mediating a life in which
wit, non-sequiturs, flashes of pathos and anguish, natural disas-
ters, old patterns of feeling (feudist, chivalric, familial, parti-

san), and a dominately good-humored, if not successfully chan-
neled, energizing are kaleidoscopically reflected in indefatigable dialogue.[22]

Natural story tellers, these characters all talk, repeating well-known tales, embellishing, denying, con-
firming, and contradicting. The reader marvels at the
energy of all these voices, their varied tones and accents,
the range of feeling and desire beneath them, the endless
surprises they can spring.[23] Talk is their speciality and
their comfort, their amusement and their preservation.
Each one has his own story-telling techniques. Little
Elvie can copy Gloria "just like Poll Parrott"; Etoyle
embroiders when she tells tales, but she is also willing to
sit and listen because she loves "to hear-tell"; Uncle Percy whispers when his turn comes, lifts his hands for
quiet, and goes into falsetto. Percy is such an effective
story teller that hearing him prompts Birdie to tell her
husband Dolphus, "Ain't Percy grand? He gets 'em all
down pat . . . I wish I was married to him. . . . He'd keep
me entertained." When Beulah launches into the story of
her parents' mysterious drowning, Ralph murmurs to
Judge Moody, "'I wish I'd had a penny for every time
I've listened to this one' . . . but Miss Beulah drove on,
and everybody listened except Gloria." Sam Dale's is the
one story they wish they never had to tell, and Lexie
Renfro's stories about her patients are so heartless that
Beulah says, "Let's not be served with any of your stories
today, Lexie." Even before Lexie begins her awful tale of
Miss Julia's last illness, Beulah has said, "That's a good
place to stop your story now, Lexie." Lexie, of course,
will not be stopped. When Gloria talks and uses an unfamiliar word, Elvie cries, "What's Normal? Don't skip
it! Tell it!" Aunt Birdie sharply rebukes Lexie for inter-
rupting Gloria: "Leave the child alone, Lexie. Nobody
asked you to help tell."

Opposite this almost nonstop talk is silence, which
finally comes when the book is nearly three-fourths

done: the narrative voice reports, "For the first time, all talk was cut off, and no baby offered to cry. Silence came traveling in on solid, man-made light. 'Now that's better,' Mrs. Moody said, 'Seems like we're back in civilization for the time being.'" Near the end of the novel when attempts to get the Moodys' car down from Banner Top are not succeeding, Judge Moody asks in exasperation, "Can't conversation ever cease?" Like silence, the written word is also opposite conversation; Miss Julia's life was symbolized by books, her letter to Judge Moody, and her will written in the old spelling-book. The Beecham and Renfro families (except for Jack's wife Gloria and for Vaughn) have little interest in reading and writing. Aunt Birdie remains puzzled that the prizes Miss Julia gave out for reading at the end of school were more books. Birdie dreaded to win. Indeed, the aunts hate books because they know the written word proceeds from solitude, from a furious need to say the truth.[24]

Place is most important in this novel, as it is in all Miss Welty's work. Banner, the community where the Renfros, the Beechams, the Stovalls, and the Comforts, as well as such lesser lights as Willy Trimble, the Broadwees, Captain Billy Bangs, and Brother Bethune, live, is rural in every sense. The time is a summer in the 1930s, and the region is the hill country of northeast Mississippi, not the rich Delta. The Depression furnishes the barest stage during which times are hardest and people have "nothing at all and yet had all the resources of their own character and situation to do what they could about their lives."[25] The impending poverty that faces the Renfro family manifests itself in dozens of ways, primarily in the extravagant new tin roof that shines in welcome as Jack returns from prison. That gesture of prosperity fades when Curly Stovall, Jack's antagonist, leans out of the truck that had been Jack's and says, "Then ask your daddy! What do you think he give me to pay for that new tin roof? To keep folks from feeling sorry for your fami-

ly." Jack's private treasure (the truck) is sacrificed for a
public display (the tin roof), an attempt to disguise reality. The 1930s were years when families hoped for a
pretty design on the cloth sacks that held flour and chick-
en feed because, once emptied, this year's sack became
this year's dress or shirt. Beulah Renfro's three girls had
dresses "made alike from the same print of flour sack,
covered with Robin Hood and his Merry Men shooting
with bow and arrow." Gloria's gift for Jack's homecoming, a store-bought shirt, was paid for with a barrelful of
pecans. Brother Bethune speaks condescendingly about
the poor: "Looks like some not too far from the sound of
my voice is going to have to go on *relief* for the first time.
Ha! Ha!" He trusts that Uncle Sam will recognize the
tastes Boone County has and keep wormy apples out of
the distribution of commodities at Christmas time. Ralph
Renfro's adamant denial of their impending economic
plight does not alter the truth of Bethune's tactless
words.

Much of the Beecham and Renfro pride is fixed in
their majestic pecan trees, which produce the sweetest,
juiciest nuts; but the newest in-law, Cleo, sees little in
them, convinced that "None of you have much, do you?"
Their poverty is not to be attributed solely to bad farm-
ing conditions and the caprices of the weather, but in
some ways to their own narrow limitations. Part of the
battle Miss Julia waged against poverty was mailing
rooted peach trees from her orchard. Her plan was to
have orchards started everywhere, one bulwark against
hard times. Percy saw no purpose in her plan. "I got a
peach tree from her, traveling through the mails. And so
did everybody on my route get one. Didn't ask for it. . . .
Why'd she waste it on me? I'm not peach-crazy." Their
stubborn resistance to education and change was willful,
but now Percy blames Miss Julia for their plight. "It's
her fault right now, we don't know as much as we might.
Stay poor as Job's turkey all our lives. She ought to made

us *stay* in school and learn some profit." Times are indeed
hard, and the Renfros may have to accept relief before
long unless Jack performs miracles with the land. Their
brave front stems from their stamina and endurance. As
Beulah says in the end, they *have* to stand it all.

This family has long been accustomed to enduring
hard times. Granny's daughter Ellen left the house with
her husband Euclid one dark night, and, heeding the
cries to stop from not one of their children nor from
Granny, they pushed forward relentlessly, not knowing
the bridge at the Bywy River was a big hole. Both
drowned, leaving seven small children behind, a multi-
responsibility which Granny and Grandpa assumed.
The reason that called the couple out and led them to
leave their large family died with them, but Granny's
stamina saw her through raising a second family. Her
generation had endured other hardships, including a cy-
clone. "'It made another case of having to start over. You
just don't quite know today how your old folks did it,'
said Mr. Renfro." Sam Dale, the darling of the seven
children, suffered a serious childhood accident and then
dashed family hopes by being killed in the war; Nathan
cut off his right hand as penance for the unjust hanging
of a black; Curtis grieved that all his sons moved away
from the farm; Noah Webster married the insensitive
Cleo; Beulah's husband Ralph could not work at full
capacity. Time passes, but conditions are still hard.
Store-bought possessions are few; with Judge and Mrs.
Moody to spend the night, there are not enough beds to
go around; the farm has languished in Jack's absence; and
Ella Fay has lost the great possession, the gold ring Granny had removed from the dead Ellen. Nevertheless, they
survive. Even though they are *losing* (verb), they are still
bravely fighting, those *losing* (participle) battles,[26] as Miss
Julia did in the schoolroom.

In spite of family troubles, poor farm crops, persistent drought, and uncertainty about the future, the spirit

of *Losing Battles* is comic; indeed, Seymour Gross sees the
novel as the culmination of Miss Welty's comic fiction.
The comedy takes almost countless forms—irony, farce,
non sequiturs, incongruities, wit—but the novel "is more
than a series of hilarious sequences."[27] With the seven
brothers and sisters and their respective families gathered
to celebrate Granny's birthday, the stage is full of steady
and energetic talkers. (Only Granny, her grandson
Nathan, and her great-grandson Vaughn have little to
say.) Beulah, the granddaughter with whom Granny
lives, oversees the reunion from the kitchen as easily as
from the porch where everybody is seated, and does so
by marching, crying, shouting, yelling, shrieking,
screaming, challenging, and scoffing. When Jack greets
his small daughter, Lady May, for the first time (he was
in prison when she was born), the child makes him feel
right at home. "She cannonballed in like a little version of
Mama." Loudness and force often make Beulah's actions
amusing, but do not diminish her goodness.

Much of the comedy comes from Aunt Cleo, who
has the candor of "a non partisan inquisitor whose quest
for the complete and probably discreditable record surpasses her tact."[28] Always blunt, Cleo comments and
asks questions indiscriminately, and with no reaction
when her words hit a sensitive spot. When Beulah introduces her three daughters, ages seven, nine, and sixteen,
Cleo makes a curious chronological judgment and
thoughtlessly comments on their hair style: "Three generations and all fixing their hair in the same pigtails.
You-all must be a mighty long ways from civilization
away up here." What Cleo wants to know about Jack is
not his state of well-being, his marriage, his child, or his
plans for the future, but why he was sent to prison. One
look at Gloria's walk and Cleo announces, "*Now* I'd know
her for a teacher anywhere." After criticizing Gloria's
bridal dress for having too much material, Cleo gets
around to a tactless question about the ceremony. "Well,

where'd you hold the wedding? Your church right on the
road? Or do you all worship off in the woods somewhere?"

Comedy in the novel occasionally reaches a farcical
level as dizzying as the antics of the Keystone Cops. To
avoid hitting Gloria, who has dashed into the road after
Lady May, Judge Moody swerves the car and ends up
straddling Banner Top. Only a tree, one of Nathan's
religious signs ("Where Will YOU Spend Eternity?"), and
Aycock Comfort (now sitting in the back seat) keep the
car from plunging over the top. In charge of the rescue
operation, Jack demonstrates dubious qualities of leadership, but is mortified at the suggestion of outside help.
Maud Eva Moody loudly insists that the car is hers and
must be brought down without a scratch. Since Jack has
had little success thus far, Mrs. Moody takes over:
"'Church people! Now they'll be my answer. . . . They'll
stop and help!' She composed a long face and moved
forward." No cars stop, and her next move is to take her
husband by the shoulders and command him: "March.
To the ends of the earth if need be. Only bring me back
somebody with the wherewithal and the gumption to get
it back for me." Adding to the farce are the Broadwees,
who appear out of the woods en masse chanting, "That
tree's gonna give," and are silenced by Mrs. Moody's
command, "Suppose you just pray." The final steps take
on cinematic features. The Buick, literally on the edge, is
tied to the truck by a tow rope held on to by a human
chain—Jack, Gloria, Beulah, Maude Eva, and the
Judge—who tug in vain. The rope snaps. Landing miraculously on a ledge, the Buick finally is brought to the
road. In the final procession is Jack, driving the school
bus towing the Buick and the truck, which now refuses
to run. Vaughn, who had appeared with the bus on his
route, rides the brake—two mules—and frequent stops
occur as the children board the bus.

At the heart of *Losing Battles* is Miss Julia Percival

Mortimer, who has touched all the adult characters in one way or another. They may have resented her urging them to be something better than they were, but they can still quote poetry and spell words, sew a seam, use a handsaw, or plant a garden because she taught them how. Her presence pervades the novel, and one senses her many disappointments and her few triumphs as well as her unshaken belief in education to the near exclusion of everything else. Unselfish, she takes milk from her cows to supplement her students' diet and tries hard to share her abundance of fruit trees, flower plants, and vegetable seeds. Resourceful and untiring, she wages war on ignorance and likes to say, "If it's going to be a case of Saint George and the Dragon, I might as well battle it left, right, front, back, center, and sideways." When her protégé, Gloria Short, announces her intention to marry Jack Renfro rather than continue to teach, Miss Julia argues, "Instead of marrying your pupil, why can't you stick to your guns and turn yourself into a better teacher and do him and the world some good?"

Like Miss Eckhart in "June Recital," Miss Julia sets her heart on molding the career of one pupil who will not be molded (neither Virgie Rainey nor Gloria Short will have their lives laid out for them). Furthermore, both teachers turn inward, to their mission of teaching, and do not stretch outward to engage in cultivating friends. They remain alone, untouched by the power of love. For all her hard work, Miss Eckhart ends up old, a little mad, and utterly alone. Likewise, in spite of the handful of students that Miss Julia has pushed out of Banner to make something of themselves, she is found dead and returned to her bed by Willy Trimble, one of her most insensitive pupils, who dispatches her with, "Down fell she. End of *her*. And her cow was calling its head off." To exclude love is to pay a considerable price and to forego much happiness.

Miss Julia may be the heart of the novel, but Jack

Jordan Renfro is its hero. The family knows he will get out of prison and be home for Granny's birthday. (He rides a mule right out of the prison, effecting his escape one day before his scheduled release.) His adventures "are a parody of those knights-errant; and his depth of character saves him from being a caricature like L'il Abner of the comic strip."[29] His return is heralded by a cacophonous medley: Aunt Nanny hides Lady May "screaming as if she herself had nearly been caught in her nightgown," the dogs' barking reaches a frantic pitch, chatterers are heard from the back porch through the house on out to the front gallery, the very floor of the house drums and sways, a pan drops from its nail onto the floor, the new tin roof "seemed to quiver with a sound like all the family spoons set to jingling in their glass," and Jack, riding a wave of dogs, leaps up the front steps, crashes his hands together, and then swings wide his arms. He has come home. Only nineteen, Jack must accept the challenge. "We're relying on Jack now. He'll haul us out of our misery." He may be proud, determined, and optimistic, but like many other heroes, he is also innocent and, in turn, somewhat foolish and naïve.[30] His outer battle of salvaging the farm is matched by the inner battle of convincing Gloria to accept her role within the large family rather than struggle to separate Jack from the Renfro household. Although Miss Julia set her hope on Gloria, and the Renfro family look to Jack to save them from economic disaster, neither Gloria nor Jack will be able to fulfill these expectations. Each has been overpraised and overrated, but they do have each other and they do respond to the power of love.

Opposite Jack is his younger brother Vaughn, who quietly lives on the edge of all the hubbub. Studious, serious, and reflective, Vaughn has always existed in Jack's shadow. "For a year and a half it has been 'Vaughn! Vaughn!' every minute, though it would turn before he knew it back into 'Jack!' again. Or would it?" As others have suggested, the prodigal son theme illus-

trates the brothers' relationship, although in this case it is
the older, not the younger, brother who has been away
and returns. To Vaughn, Jack is the center of his un-
happiness, the cause of his taking second place to everybody. "'Without Jack, nothing would be no trouble at
all.' Vaughn spoke it out." When all the noises of the
reunion are stilled and moonlight covers the house with
quiet, Vaughn silently goes with Bet the mule, and with
no fanfare pulls the school bus out of the ditch. Once
back on the road, the bus engine runs "for Vaughn just as
any engine in the world ought to do"; and he leaves the
bus in place for his morning route. Slipping past all the
sleepers again, Vaughn is distressed when Granny
awakens and, not knowing who he is, invites him to her
bed. After spending the rest of the night in the barn,
Vaughn has already hitched the wagon and taken Judge
and Mrs. Moody to Banner Top before Jack and Gloria
even stir. Morning light shows with certainty that the
reunion is over and that life has returned to its normal
level, a level that indicates Vaughn's position in the family. He tries to say something in the kitchen about de-
livering the Moodys, but is interrupted.

"Well, don't sit down—you haven't got time to eat breakfast,
Vaughn Renfro. Scoot! Up, the rest of you children! You've
got your chores to finish and then school to track for, and
Vaughn's got the teacher to tell he's misput the bus. There's
only one new pair of shoes to be ruined, there's a mercy." . . .

"Vaughn'll catch a whipping at the door. I'll give him one
myself when he gets back this evening, with a little extra for the
hay he's lost his daddy," said Miss Beulah.

"If everybody hadn't wanted the gathering and all to wait
on Jack!" Vaughn cried, "I could have had the hay saved!"

"It was what you felt called on to cut and leave laying in
the field, Contrary, that's out yonder to spoil now. . . ."

"Feed the stock. Lead the cows to pasture, Vaughn," said
Mr. Renfro. "You heard your mother. The reunion is over
with."

"I ain't done anything," said Vaughn.

"Then keep still," said Uncle Nathan.

Vaughn's frustrations culminate when he goes to feed the pig, all the remains of the reunion now reduced to distasteful refuse. The family could watch as

> Vaughn was feeding the pig. They had only to turn their heads to see all the refuse of yesterday, corncobs, eggshells, chicken bones, chicken trimmings, chicken heads, and the fish heads, all jumping together in the blue wash of clabber, all going down. Rusty looked back at them, with tiny eyes. He had the old, mufflered face of winter this morning and fed sobbing with greed, champing against blasts he was never going to feel.

Vaughn's last displacement comes when Jack commandeers the school bus, demoting Vaughn from driving the bus to riding the mules. "'It's no blooming fair,' said Vaughn, accepting it." His last humiliation comes when he finally unloads his passengers at the schoolhouse, and faces the teacher he is so ready to worship. At that moment the other pupils cry, "Vaughn's big brother he's been to the pen." The importance given to Vaughn's relatively minor role compared with Jack's is underscored by the manner in which the moonlight episode is told. The narration "is stylistically unlike any other part of the novel; the prose is reminiscent of, for example, 'First Love'—mysterious, evocative, resistant to paraphrase, as if it were a projection of and a tribute to a sensibility still mute."[31] Jack may hear his family say, "Hail the conquering hero come," but Vaughn sees that the whole problem created by the family, and by Jack himself, is in believing that he is invincible. "Could Jack take a fall from highest places and nobody be man enough to say so?"

The range, depth, and sheer number of details reflect Miss Welty's care and pleasure in the book. Flowers appear in abundance—cannas, red salvia, lemon lily, prince's feather, althea bush, dahlias; fruits are seemingly endless and delectable: "a cigar box full of late figs, laid closely, almost bruising each other, in the leaves and purple and heavy as turned-over sacks, with pink bubbles rising to the top and a drunk wasp that had come with them from Peerless." The carefully chosen list of birthday presents for Granny gives a miniature history of the entire family, their tastes, and their preferences:

Her lap was holding a new white cup and saucer, and on the ground around her rested everything else she had untied from the strings and unshucked from its wrappings, all their presents—a pillow of new goose feathers, a pint of fresh garden sass, a soda-box full of sage, a foot-tub full of fresh-dug, blooming-size hyacinth bulbs, three worked pincushions, an envelope full of blood-red Indian peach seeds, a prayer-plant that had by now folded its leaves, a Joseph's coat, a double touch-me-not, a speckled geranium, and an Improved Boston fern wrapped in bread paper, a piece of cut-glass from the mail order house given by Uncle Noah Webster, a new apron, the owl lamp, and, chewing a hambone, the nine-month-old, already treeing, long-eared Blue-tick coonhound pup that any of her great-grandchildren would come and take out hunting for her any time she was ready. And there behind her, spread over her chair and ready to cloak her, was "The Delectable Mountains."

The surface of Miss Welty's fiction, as Louis Rubin has remarked, "is always deceptively mundane, matter-of-fact, usually funny."[32] That surface often takes on a lyric quality, too, that moves the novel beyond the moment-by-moment talking of the Beecham kin into an element of nature, a move to which the more sensitive respond. Miss Lexie holds forth with details about her bed-ridden patient, Mr. Huff, and cocks her ankle to announce, "These are his socks . . . I'm still busy wearing out some of his socks for him." In contrast to Lexie's strident tone comes the narrative voice saying

A thrush was singing. As they all fell quiet, except for Miss Lexie dragging her own chair back to the table, its evening song was heard.

Granny heard that out too. Then she whispered, and Miss Beulah put her head down.

"I'm ready to go home now."

Miss Beulah put her arms around her. Granny, as well as she was able, kept from being held. "Granny, you *are* home," said Miss Beulah, gazing into her grandmother's face. . . .

"Then," said Granny, "I think I'd be right ready to accept a birthday present from somebody." . . .

"You've had your presents, Granny. You've already had every single one," said Miss Beulah softly.

Granny covered her eyes. Her fingers trembled, the backs of her hands showed their blotches like pansy faces pressed into the papery skin.

"Just look around you," said Miss Beulah. "And you've thanked everybody, too."

Then Granny dropped her hands, and she and Miss Beulah looked at each other, each face as griefstricken as the other.

The song of the thrush fills Granny's memory, confusing the present with the past, making the just-completed act an event of the future until the present moment again takes control, bringing with it the reality of old age and impending death.

Losing Battles is a major novel; resisting summary and paraphrase, it portrays universal concerns by focusing on life in Banner, Mississippi. Miss Welty is keenly aware that "if the Old South produced anything of note in the American experience, it was the conviction that living itself is an art which requires careful fostering."[33] The meagerness of their possessions in no way matches the richness of living these characters experience, a richness conveyed through every page of *Losing Battles*. As Louis Rubin notes, "What it provides, for those willing to take part, is delight ending in wisdom."[34]

4

~·~·~·~·~·~·~·~·~·~·~·~·~·~·~·~·~·~·

Vortexes of Quiet

In *The Eye of the Story*, Miss Welty concludes an autobiographical piece, "The Little Store," with a paragraph that gives insight into the eight stories collected in *The Wide Net and Other Stories* (1943):

We weren't being sent to the neighborhood grocery for facts of life, or death. But of course those are what we were on the track of, anyway. With the loaf of bread and the Cracker Jack prize, I was bringing home the intimations of pride and disgrace, and rumors and early news of people coming to hurt one another, while others practiced for joy—storing up a portion for myself of the human mystery.

The human mystery dominates *The Wide Net*. Although only two years separated that volume from the earlier *A Curtain of Green*, many critics reacted as if light years had intervened. To be sure, *A Curtain of Green* in no way prepared readers for *The Wide Net*. Jean Stafford, writing in the *Partisan Review*, said: "One can only hope that the talents which executed 'The [*sic*] Petrified Man' and 'Why I Live at the P.O.' will awaken from this stumbling sleep."[1] Other reviewers found the landscape imprecise, the language often vague, and with few exceptions, the humor missing. In short, the stories in *The Wide Net* are radically different from the earlier ones. More reflective and introspective, more meditative and questioning, they are *vortexes of quiet* in which the human mystery is

taken into account, in which metaphysical questions are
raised but not always answered. "Livvie" is the single
story reminiscent of the earlier work, and many readers
were far more comfortable with Solomon's bottle tree
and Livvie's visit with Miss Baby Marie, the door-to-
door cosmetic seller, than they were with William Wallace Jamison in "The Wide Net," or Josie in "The
Winds." William Wallace's dive to the very heart of the
Pearl River brings about an unspoken renewal of life and
a reunion with his pregnant wife Hazel and the studied
reflections of Josie mark the beginning of her separating
the fantasies of childhood from the realities of imminent
adulthood. Reviewing the book for *The Nation*, Diana
Trilling never questioned Miss Welty's dedication as a
writer, but called *The Wide Net* a book of ballets, not
of stories. Leo Lerman, writing in the *New York Herald
Tribune*, however, found the volume a great success.

She writes of Natchez, the old Trace, poor whites, Negroes on
remote and isolated bits of soil wrested from jungle and river,
Southern aristocracy fallen from fashion and high estate,
moldering mansions, forgotten villages, and the Mississippi
flows eternally through her pages, but although her idiom is
richly native and her people and environment are indubitably
Deep South she interprets and records verity, universal verity,
by implication and with humor.[2]

The Trilling review, nevertheless, set the tone, and at
least in part prompted Robert Penn Warren's 1944 article
in the *Kenyon Review* ("The Love and the Separateness
in Miss Welty's Fiction"),[3] a resounding defense of the
direction her fiction had taken.

Two of the stories, "First Love" and "A Still Moment," show the "complex process by which Miss Welty
assimilates, selects, and transforms historical matter into
satisfying aesthetic forms."[4] As important as Miss Welty's correlation of historical fact is, and as effective as the
historical figures Aaron Burr and Harman Blennerhas-

sett are, the intriguing character is Joel Mayes, a deaf boy of twelve. His lonely world is depicted with haunting poignancy. Virginia was the site of his childhood, but his parents took him much farther south; those parents "vanished in the forest, were cut off from him, and in spite of his last backward look, dropped behind." This horror is soon followed by another. Rescued by Old Man McCaleb and joined to his party, Joel soon learns what it is like to hide from the Indians: "Crouched by his bush, Joel had cried . . . He gasped and put his mouth quicker than thought against the earth. He took leaves in his mouth." Left by McCaleb at the inn in Natchez, Joel gets room and board in exchange for his services as bootblack, an occupation Miss Welty brings to reality. By habit Joel wakes late in the night, takes his candle, and fetches the mud-caked boots of sleeping men. The solitude of the hour and the task does not bother him—"he was alone in the way he liked to be." His task is not without danger, for sleeping men sometimes shake him hard, reacting from the horror of nightmare. The great adventure of Joel's life, however, is the unexplained presence of Aaron Burr and Harman Blennerhassett in his small room, as they hold earnest, late-night discussions which center, of course, around Burr's conspiracy trial, notices of which Joel was given by the innkeeper to post on the saloon mirror. Without actually knowing the two men, Joel's "love went out to the talkers. He would not have known how to hold it back." Joel watches Burr's every mood, sets food and drink in front of him (saved from his own supper or stolen from the kitchen), and once when Burr has fallen asleep across the table, Joel clasps the man's hand until he sees the words of nightmare cease.

Two episodes movingly depict the private world of the deaf. Walking on a cold January day, Joel watches puffs of breath come from people's mouths as they exchange greetings or stop to talk, and his dark face "showed its secret desire. It was marvelous to him when the infinite designs of speech became visible information on the air." Late one night, Blennerhassett's young wife enters the room and plays the violin, creating in Joel "a sensation of pain, the ends of his fingers were stinging. At first he did not realize that he had heard the sounds of her song, the only thing he had ever heard." Speech and music are lost worlds to the deaf lad, yet he mysteriously responds to them.

In the end, Burr escapes his trial, riding out of Natchez in a somewhat humiliating disguise. His departure robs Joel of his unspoken first love and leaves him in the grip of the bitter cold (that engulfs all but one day of the action), grieving for all his losses: "He saw that the bodies of the frozen birds had fallen out of the trees, and he fell down and wept for his father and mother, to whom he had not said goodbye."

"A Still Moment" brings three men to a chance meeting by a great forked oak where they are all struck by the beauty of a snowy heron feeding, and through this brief encounter, they reveal their innermost natures. First introduced is Lorenzo Dow, whose burning desire to save souls blinds him to human love. This he finds effortless only from a distance (his wife, Peggy, is far away in Massachusetts). James Murrell, the outlaw and self-declared devil, emerges from the cane brake to ride along with Dow, his next intended victim. At sunset when they dismount at the tree, Murrell's long *dark* coat and his *dark* face still *darkening* contrast with the appearance of the third man, James Audubon, who approaches "*lightly* on the wilderness floor, disturbing nothing in his *lightness* [italics added]." Caught in this moment, the three reflect their own fanaticism: Dow to save all souls, Murrell to destroy all men, and Audubon to record all life that fills this world. Transfixed by the sight of the heron, each responds in character: to Dow the bird symbolizes God's love become visible; to Murrell the moment brings his triumphant vision of proud leadership

over slaves, brigands, and outcasts, flaunting as he
strides "an awesome great picture of the Devil colored on
a banner"; to Audubon it is a moment of minute observation (when the heron feeds, it muddies the water with its
foot) and of endless questions about the structure of life.

To paint the heron, Aubudon shoots it, the shot
resounding within each man's inner self. Shaken by the
deed, Dow muses upon the idea of love and separateness
and of the futile task of explaining time and separateness back to God. Murrell resists the tempting beauty of
the bird and reacts instead to "a dark voice that rose up to
overcome the wilderness voice, or was one with it." The
gentle, light-filled Audubon picks up the still warm bird
and pockets it, knowing that the best he will ever do is to
paint "a dead thing and not a live thing, never the essence, only a sum of parts." This brief, still moment discloses each man's heart, but with no confession and with
no real understanding of each other.

Although in strikingly different ways, "Asphodel,"
"The Winds," "Livvie," and "At the Landing" also ex-
plore the human mystery. The Greek trappings in
"Asphodel"—the house Asphodel is a golden ruin with
six Doric columns, and the three old maids (Cora, Irene,
and Phoebe) are on an idyllic picnic furnished with dain-
ties of meat and cordial—underscore the tragedy of Miss
Sabina. The old maids retell Miss Sabina's story end-
lessly; and for all the humor of her ex-husband, Mr. Don
McInnis (not Greek *at all*), appearing buck-naked before
the old maids, and the goats chasing the ladies in their
horse-driven cart away from Asphodel (the ladies throwing food from the last picnic basket as appeasement and
calling, "Here billy-goats!" as they flee), Miss Sabina's
tragic life is still the story that is told. Past the age of
attracting suitors, Miss Sabina was forced to marry
McInnis, her father's choice. She bore three children
(each of whom dies tragically in young adulthood), drove
out her unfaithful husband, and dressed in heavy,

ancient, ill-fitting brocades and a huge black wig, endowed and ruled the little town. She gave a museum and the water works just as she set wedding dates and named babies for the citizens. Her enemy was the small post office, symbol of the present, of the real world, and of messages bearing love and promises. Her life ended after a vicious attack on the post office; she demanded entrance, destroyed everything in sight, and finally fell dead, "her wig fallen from her head and her face awry like a mask."

The mixture of fantasy and reality sets "Asphodel" apart from Josie's late night coming of age during an equinoctial storm ("The Winds"), and from Jenny's leaving the house of her grandfather to follow the strange adventure of love at the hands of Billy Floyd ("At the Landing"). Her search for Floyd leads to her violation by the river men; she had searched for him because "the shock of love had brought a trembling to her fingers, and made her stumble on the stair, though all the time she was driven on." Livvie's story is of a May-January marriage. Married to Solomon, who brought her to his neat but isolated house, Livvie has endured loneliness; now as she watches Solomon die, she is sorely tempted by his young field hand, Cash McCord. Just returned from Natchez, Cash is, he says, ready for Easter, a veritable rainbow of color:

Starting at the bottom with his pointed shoes, he began to look up, lifting his peg-top pants the higher to see fully his bright socks. His coat long and wide and leaf-green he opened like doors to see his high-up tawny pants and his pants he smoothed downward from the points of his collar, and he wore a luminous baby-pink satin shirt. At the end, he reached gently above his wide platter-shaped round hat, the color of a plum, and one finger touched at the feather, emerald green, blowing in the spring winds.

The outcome of a May-January marriage has long been predicted. The dying Solomon acknowledges both that

Livvie was too young to be his wife and that he selfishly
has kept her away from people her own age. His dignity
in life and in death, however, lifts the story from the
stereotypic and merely humorous. Although Livvie does
weep over the dying man and accepts his silver watch,
the symbol of his orderly and prosperous life, she leaves
the death room to join Cash. As is often true in Miss
Welty's fiction, the power of love leads the characters on;
Livvie drops Solomon's watch to the floor, and her union
with Cash is heralded by the full song of a bird and the
bursting light of spring.

Unlike the other stories in the collection, "The Purple Hat" has been described as extreme, grosteque, surrealistic, Gothic, a ghost story, and supernatural. Set in a
New Orleans gambling house, the Palace of Pleasure, the
story tells the strange tale of a large, middle-aged woman
who meets her young lover in the gambling house each
day at five o'clock. A dominant object is her ridiculous,
monstrous purple hat, with its curious glass vial and
jeweled hat pin. A fat man, whose job is to watch the
gamblers from the catwalk, tells of also watching the
woman in the purple hat for these thirty years. He has
twice seen her murdered and thinks now she may be a
ghost. Keeping his listeners at the bar spellbound, the fat
man says at the end, "Up on the catwalk you get the
feeling now and then that you could put out your finger
and make a change in the universe." His imagined power, however, does not extend to his being able to answer
the bartender's question: "Is she a real ghost?" Miss Welty
has remarked that she wished she had not written the
story. "I saw it dramatized last year, an off-Broadway
thing, which only brought home to me its failings. It was
just an odd story I wrote in an odd moment, about something I don't know much about: gambling. But I really
meant it to be no more than a kind of playful ghost story.
. . . I wasn't trying to be allegorical or anything else."[5]

The title story, "The Wide Net," relates a detailed
ritual "celebrating a summer king's renewal of a goddess

figure."[6] William Wallace Jamison does not understand why his pregnant wife Hazel acts the way she does, and he stays out all night drinking to make his protest. Returning home, he finds Hazel's note saying she has drowned herself in the Pearl River. The ritual begins as William Wallace summons his friend Virgil, gets the wide net and its owner Doc, and accumulates a sufficient number of invited and uninvited helpers. Punctuated with eel-wrestling, alligator processions, and fish catches, the ritual reaches a climax when William Wallace dives deep into the river, discovering there "the real, the true trouble that Hazel had fallen into, about which words in a letter could not speak . . . she had been filled to the brim with elation." Like Marjorie in "Flowers for Marjorie," Hazel is filled with "the elation that comes of great hopes and changes" from her pregnancy, and William Wallace in his dive finds out that their difficulty is nothing but the old trouble all face in similar circumstances, and emerges holding, root and all, a green plant. His sign of renewal in hand, all William Wallace lacks is reunion with Hazel, who, as Doc has known all along, was not in the river at all. Before they all gorge themselves on fish, William Wallace must heroically wrestle the King of Snakes. The only remaining test for him is getting past Hazel's formidable mother as the river party, strings of fish in hand, make their triumphant entry into Dover. The dancing, diving, eating, sleeping, and marching are done, and William Wallace returns home to find Hazel. "It was the same as any other chase in the end."

As Anne Masserand has pointed out, the journey is a frequent theme in Miss Welty's fiction, and certainly in *The Wide Net*. Joel's journey to Natchez; the chance meeting of Dow, Murrell, and Audubon; the picnic journey of Cora, Irene, and Phoebe; Josie's mental journey into fantasy with Cornella, the older girl across the street; Jenny's search for Billy Floyd; Livvie's journey to Solo-

mon's house and back again ("Livvie" was originally entitled "Livvie Is Back"); and William Wallace Jamison's
journey to the depth of the Pearl River combine to
make a catalog of adventures. Their journeys have
brought these characters a way to link with vital forces,
to meet experiences, and to gain knowledge of themselves, other people, and perhaps the world.[7] Although
The Wide Net as a whole has not been as popular with
readers or critics as others of Miss Welty's works, it
nevertheless succeeds in recording universal verity
through the lives of radically different characters, in
settings and situations that move between reality and
fantasy.

Joyce Carol Oates in a brief article makes especially
astute observations when she says that Miss Welty
"baffles our expectations" because

. . . she presents the distortions of life in the context of ordinary, even chatty life; she frightens us. I have no doubt that
her intentions are not to frighten anyone, or to make particular
judgments on life, but the effect of her fiction is indeed fright-
ening. It is the bizarre combination of a seemingly boundless
admiration for feminine nonsense—family life, food, relatives,
conversations, eccentric old people—and a sharp, penetrating
eye for the seams of this world, through which a murderous
light shines.[8]

One may well quarrel with the phrase "feminine nonsense," but the combination of the five elements listed
accounts for a good portion of Miss Welty's subject matter. The Fairchild clan (of Fairchilds, Mississippi) in *Delta Wedding* is certainly a study of family life, richly aug-
mented with food (they never want to leave the dining
room, which has rocking chairs as well as dining-table
chairs), relatives, conversations, and eccentric old people. The family is appealing, and Miss Oates suggests
that even the most impatient and unsympathetic of readers at last is charmed by them. The appeal and charm

may lie in the vicarious experience of the reader, who is able "to participate in that sense of family which few readers in a restless age are lucky enough to experience directly."[9]

Delta Wedding begins on September 10, 1923, a year chosen because no natural disaster beset the Mississippi Delta that year, and no war disrupted domestic life. The uneventfulness of that year, Miss Welty said, "would allow me to concentrate on the people without any undue outside influences; I wanted to write a story that showed the solidity of this family and the life that went on on a small scale in a world of its own. So the date was chosen by necessity."[10] The time setting assured that the men were home and that family tranquility was threatened only by internal affairs, not external catastrophes. The year 1923 in a sense insulated Shellmound, the Grove, and Marmion—the three dwellings on the Fairchild plantation—and prompted critics to label the novel pastoral. Indeed, family life as a whole seems too idyllic and good to be true. The real threats to Fairchild happiness seem absurd to the outsider—Aunt Tempe's daughter Mary Denis has married a Yankee, a Buchanan, and moved to Illinois; Dabney, the bride of *Delta Wedding*, marries Troy Flavin, a hill man and overseer of the Fairchild plantation; and Robbie Reid has left her husband George Fairchild, who does not deserve such treatment according to the relatives.

The sheer size of the family is formidable. Battle Fairchild reigns at Shellmound, the primary house, with his wife Ellen Dabney from Mitchum Corners, Virginia, and their eight children—Shelley, Dabney, India, Roy, Orrin, Little Battle, Ranny, and Bluet. (Ellen is at the moment pregnant with their tenth child; she miscarried a baby son, a loss apparently caused by the turmoil when the gin burned.) Added to this number at Shellmound are the great-aunts, Shannon and Mac, two fascinating old ladies. In 1890, when Shannon and Mac were two poor Civil War widows, their brother James Fairchild (who completed building Marmion that very year) accused Old Ronald McBane of not protecting his landing, from which cotton was shipped to his gin. McBane denied the charge and challenged James to a duel, during which he shot and killed him. Shortly after, James's wife, Laura Allen, died of grief. Shannon and Mac were thus left to raise eight children (Denis, Battle, George, Tempe, Annie Laurie, Rowena, Jim Allen [female], and Primrose), the oldest of whom was twelve. Furthermore, Aunt Mac was prepared to raise another brood should anything happen to Battle and Ellen. (Miss Welty used a similar family situation in *Losing Battles*, when Granny and Grandpa Vaughn were obliged to raise their grandchildren.) The other residents at Shellmound are guests: Laura McRaven, whose mother, Annie Laurie Fairchild, has recently died and Mary Lamar Mackay of Lookback Plantation, Dabney's best friend. A host of blacks in the house and in the fields completes the total household.

Living nearby at the Grove, George's house, are Aunt Primrose and Aunt Jim Allen. Marmion, vacant since the 1890 tragedy, is to be occupied finally by Dabney and her husband, Troy Flavin. Of Battle's brothers and sisters, Denis, Rowena, and Annie Laurie are dead; Tempe married Pinck Summers and moved to Inverness, and George, the favored one after Denis's death, marries Robbie Reid (a match below Fairchild expectations) and practices law in Memphis. If this much family is not enough, family portraits at the Grove are constant reminders of the ancestors who came and tamed the wilderness, and now Mary Denis Summers Buchanan, Tempe's daughter, has children—Lady Clare, who attends the wedding, and an infant son, George, born just days before the wedding. Aunt Shannon's mind slips in and out of the past as she converses with Fairchilds living and dead, all important. In sheer numbers, the family fills a large stage.

Action in *Delta Wedding* centers around family events: Dabney's rather sudden plans to marry Troy Flavin, the visit of nine-year-old Laura McRaven, the temporary disruption of George Fairchild's marriage, and Ellen's pregnancy. The domestic hubbub over Dabney's wedding is considerable: box after box arrives from Memphis bearing everything from the wedding cake ("Only God knew if it is digestible!") to the shepherdesses' crooks the bridesmaids will carry. Curtains are washed and starched and dried, windows cleaned, floors waxed, silver polished, a rehearsal dinner planned and cooked, countless dresses ironed, parties attended, and gifts acknowledged. All these activities are attended to while the father of the bride continues to question the wisdom of the match.

Wedding gifts to Dabney are some measure of the family's affection. Aunt Jim Allen and Aunt Primrose urge her to select anything from their parlor, but when she chooses a flower bowl that has neither age nor family association to commend it, they give her instead the night light that has been, Aunt Primrose said, "company as early as I can remember—when Papa and Mama died." It had kept Civil War wives company as they waited their husbands' return. Lighted, the little lamp provides warm tea if the top part is made ready; its main body, however, reveals a discomforting picture: over the town with "trees, towers, people, windowed houses, and a bridge, over the clouds and stars and moon and sun, you saw a redness glow and the little town was all on fire, even to the motion of fire which came from the candle flame drawing." George has brought Dabney a sorrel filly with a flax mane and Memphis champagne for the reception; Aunt Tempe's gift is a forty-piece luncheon set; and from Uncle Pinck, a new Pierce-Arrow. The Dabney cousins in Virginia did not come, but sent "an outrageous number" of Bohemian wine glasses. Troy's little mother in the mountains did not have sufficient notice to make Dabney a bridal quilt, so she sent her own quilts, which Troy insists now be refolded and put "on a long table with that other conglomeration for folks to come see." In addition, the aunts cook and bake and arrange flowers and sew lace mitts throughout the days.

Household activity centers around cooking and eating, usually enormous meals in the dining room and in the kitchen, where new meals start before old ones are finished. The family celebrates Battle's birthday outdoors with a barbecue, and to welcome the bridal pair home, they picnic by the riverside. Using Aunt Mashula's recipe, Ellen makes George's favorite coconut cake, Primrose and Jim Allen have a guinea fowl dinner for him at the Grove, Jim Allen spends a whole day making mints for the wedding (better by far than the store-bought ones from Memphis), Roxie serves lemonade, mint tea, and plates of cake, and Ellen leaves a sugar almond by Bluet's pillow (a fairy's gift after her nap). To comfort Laura, Little Battle brings her a cold biscuit and ham, and Battle likes to end his evening meal with a cherry bounce. The conviviality wherever they gather is a significant part of their lives.

Talking and story telling also occupy much of their attention, for "all of them told happenings like narrations, chronological and careful, as if the ear of the world listened and wished to know surely." The tales about Mary Shannon, great-great-grandfather George, and especially Denis, are told and retold. A recent episode—George dislodged Maureen's foot from the railroad trestle just as the train stopped right in front of them—is repeated or analyzed at least seven times in the novel, and raises the questions: Who is worthy of sacrifice? And who is capable of making one? Ellen, a little clairvoyant, puts Bluet to sleep with narrations of her own dreams. Objects like the night light, a cake recipe, Mashula's dulcimer, grandfather's dueling pistols, or Ellen's garnet pin have histories that are repeated, that are part of the family. Spirited talking is not confined to the Fairchilds, however. When Robbie leaves George, she comes back to the Fairchilds' store, where she had worked, and is confronted by Troy, who urges her to go to Shellmound, and by a customer, Miss Mayo. Troy reports that George is lying in the hammock at Shellmound, and Robbie, not as successful as Hazel Jamison in "The Wide Net," cries, "I thought he might drag the river, even." The brief conversation that follows shows that the Fairchilds think best men at weddings should have dignified names and respectable occupations and reveals Miss Mayo as a woman who easily juxtaposes life's tragedies with mundane matters.

"Drag which river? Why, Dabney wanted George here, is why he's here," Troy said, looking down at her in concern. "*Dabney* sent for him. He's my what-you-call-it—best man. They didn't care for Buster Daggett, that friend of mine over at the ice and coal."

"Buster Daggett, I don't wonder," remarked Miss Mayo. "Robbie, did I hear you'd run away, and George Fairchild used to beat you unmercifully in Memphis? Cut me off a yard of black sateen, child, you're right at it."

Eccentric characters bring humor and pathos to the novel and reveal as well some of the family's customs, mores, and taboos. Their speech and action form a mirror of the family life. Displeased that banks no longer give a lady new bills, Aunt Mac, to Troy's utter amazement, washes and irons the money for the plantation payroll. Aunt Primrose is irritated that Dabney and India do not know Maureen is Aunt Mac's real name: "It made her nervous for people not to keep their kinfolks and their tragedies straight." India, age ten, shocks Aunt Primrose and Aunt Jim Allen by asking Dabney if she plans to take the night light on her honeymoon. "'Little girls don't talk about honeymoons,' said Aunt Jim Allen. 'They don't ask their sisters questions, it's not a bit

nice.'" Aunt Shannon dwells in happiness and superior-
ity over Mac. In Shannon's delicate mental state, the past
and the dead are one, giving her access not only to their
brothers killed in the Civil War, but "as well to James
killed only thirty-three years ago in the duel, to her husband Lucian Miles and even to Aunt Mac's husband
Duncan Laws," whom she addresses as "'Duncan
dearie.'" Dr. Murdoch (who had put himself, not Ellen,
to sleep with his new gas contraption when Shelley was
born) meets Shelley, India, and Laura when they all pass
the cemetery. To the girls' discomfort, he predicts which
Fairchild will have children and calculates the available
graves in the family plot.

"Look. Dabney and that fellow she's marrying will have three
or four at the least. That will give them room, over against the
Hunters—have to take up your rose bush." He wheeled about.
"Primrose and Jim Allen naturally go here, in line with Rowena
and What's-his-name that was killed, and his wife. An easy two
here. George and the Reid girl probably won't have children—
he doesn't strike me as a family man."

Although Tempe Fairchild Summers is younger than the
great-aunts and Dr. Murdoch, she is a wonderfully
eccentric character, an early and less abrasive version of
Aunt Cleo and of Maud Eva Moody in *Losing Battles*. Her
entrance to Shellmound is enough to show that Tempe is
in charge. "Aunt Tempe, in a batik dress and a vibrating-
ly large hat, entered (keeping time) and kissed all the
jumping children. Then she straightened up from her
kisses and admonitions and looked quickly around the
parlor, as if to catch it before it could compose itself."
Tempe despairs when she cannot control things, her
great defeat having come when her daughter Mary Denis
married "a Yankee that wants his windows washed three
times a week." Her temporary comfort—Mary Denis's
new baby favors Tempe—is short-lived because that
baby also "has Mr. Buchanan's Titian hair, Mr. Buchan-

an's the same Yankee he ever was, demands the impossible. . . . Oh, the mortification of *life*, Ellen!" She is a
warm, domineering, delightful, *and* eccentric character.

As M. E. Bradford has recently written, "the ortho-
dox view of the book, perhaps designed to protect it from
guilt by association, argues that it is not about the
South."[11] Quoting Andrew Lytle, Bradford says that the
Fairchild family is *the* family, another name for the
South, the institution of southern life. And to see this
family whole, we are shown how they live, what they
value and fear, what they become in their old age.
Deaths, unsuitable marriages, and changing social conditions are evidence that the Fairchild world is vulnerable;
the family is subject to change and things will not remain
frozen in the past or in the present.

In *Losing Battles*, there are no black characters, Miss
Welty explained, because Banner was set in the poverty-
stricken, red clay hills of northeast Mississippi, where
there were no plantations and no black people. Yet, she
reminded an interviewer, there is an essential incident in
Losing Battles that involves a black: an innocent sawmill
black is hanged for a murder Nathan Beecham committed. On the other hand, *Delta Wedding* is filled with
black characters—Roxie, Sudie, Vi'let, Little Uncle,
Pinchy, Juju, Sylvanus, Man-Son, Little Matthew,
Lethe, Bitsy, Howard, Big Baby, Sue Ellen, Oneida,
and Ernest—who run the kitchen and the yard, the cottonfields and the barn. The reader is never brought particularly close to any one of them, and as characters they
remain more servants than individuals. Without embark-
ing on lectures or declamations, Miss Welty exposes
some ragged seams in the Fairchild world and clearly
shows that violence and disorder exist despite the surface
tranquility of the household. Dabney remembers years
ago watching George separate two young black boys who
were fighting each other with open knives. Years later,
sent to summon Troy to the wedding rehearsal, Shelley

enters the overseer's office and sees Root M'Hook, a field hand, with an ice pick, and Juju and two other blacks, one with slashed cheeks. Troy warns that he will shoot if the ice pick moves; the man's arm vibrates and aims, and Troy shoots. "Root fell back, crying out and waving at him." Two others pull Root through the door, and the tension breaks as Troy offers to pick buckshot out of Big Baby's seat. Shelley is calmly told to jump over the blood if she wants to get out.

The trouble Troy settles is over Pinchy, the black girl who has gone through some unknown crisis during the novel, with no one to help or understand her. Wild-eyed and sweaty, she takes refuge one noon in the cotton shed, only to be ordered out by Robbie Reid, who has been walking from Fairchilds' store to Shellmound in the heat of the day. Robbie wants the shade for herself and pays no attention to the suffering Pinchy. By Dabney's wedding day, however, Pinchy has been restored to her senses and resumes her duties, setting the table and swatting the flies. We never know precisely what she suffered or what the effects of her ordeal will be.

A second bleak episode concerns the runaway girl Ellen encounters in the wood. When she discovers the girl is white, Ellen associates her with Robbie Reid; both are runaways of a sort. Three times the girl denies any knowledge of the lost pin Ellen says she is hunting. Struck by the girl's natural beauty, so unlike her own daughters, Ellen tries to clarify her words to the girl. "I wasn't speaking about any little possession to you. I suppose I was speaking about good and bad, maybe. I was speaking about men—men, our lives. But you don't know who I am." When Ellen adds that she won't try to stop her, the girl answers back, "You couldn't stop me," and momentarily takes the adult role. "A half-smile, sweet and incredibly maternal, passed over her face. It made what she said seem teasing and sad, final and familiar, like the advice a mother is bound to give her girls." Ellen points out the way to the Memphis road. When George reports that he, too, met the girl, and that he took her to the old Argle gin and slept with her, Ellen responds internally, but voices no recrimination. As the photographer snaps the bridal picture at the end of the novel, the runaway girl is mentioned a third time, now the reported victim of a train accident. Her appearance was brief but crucial, revealing the sensual side of the gallant and courtly George and reminding Ellen, that venerable matriarch, that she cannot control the decisions of others—Dabney *is* marrying red-haired Troy Flavin, the overseer, and Shelley is smoking a Fatima and writing in her diary, "Sometimes I believe we live most privately just when things are most crowded, like in the Delta, like for a wedding." The girl is evidence to Ellen that Shellmound is not the whole world or even the whole South. Not all daughters are loved, spoiled, and protected; not all escape destruction.

Published in the same year as Carson McCullers's *A Member of the Wedding* (1946), *Delta Wedding* was often compared with that novel by reviewers, but the similarities are slight. As John Alexander Allen suggests, "the principal subject of *Delta Wedding* is the intrusion of the outside world upon the changeless demi-paradise of Shellmound,"[12] but that protected world has always been haunted by past tragedies. The Civil War left Aunt Shannon and Aunt Mac's generation poor and virtually defenseless, with brothers and husbands killed. James survived, only to die in a foolish duel at a time when no romance surrounded such events. Unspoken, but not forgotten, is the trauma of Ellen's childhood: when she was nine, her mother ran away to England and another man, staying "three years before she came back." "She took up her old life and everything in the household went on as before. Like an act of God, passion went unexplained and undenied—just a phenomenon." The Fairchilds are a charming and loving family; they greet each other and their visitors with hugs and kisses; they are for their time a veritable island, a demi-paradise. Miss Welty has said that *Delta Wedding* is not a novel about the "Old South," a term, she added, that has a connotation of something unreal and not quite straightforward. For all their happiness, the protected life of the Fairchild clan is yielding not only to the social change symbolized in husbands who are Yankees or hillborn overseers and a wife who is just Old Man Swanson's granddaughter, but also to other intrusions from the world outside. Although there is more comic richness in *Losing Battles* and more earnest reflection in *The Optimist's Daughter*, *Delta Wedding* retains an important place in Miss Welty's work. It was her first full-length novel, and it did portray a part of the South on the brink of social change.

In 1955, the year *The Bride of Innisfallen* was published, Miss Welty wrote a commentary (reprinted in *The Eye of the Story* as "Writing and Analyzing a Story") on the writing of short stories in general, and of "No Place for You, My Love" in particular. The individual author's stories carry his or her own signature, Miss Welty said, but he or she shares much in common with countless other authors. "For the source of the short story is usually lyrical. And all writers speak from, and speak to, emotions eternally the same in all of us; love, pity, terror do not show favorites or leave any of us out." The seven stories in this collection share that lyric source, their plots are less definite than those in earlier stories, climaxes are inner revelations rather than overt action or explicit statement, and the stories as a whole give the reader a "dominant impression rather than a clear rational plan."[13]

Four of the stories are set in the South: "No Place for You, My Love" in New Orleans and in the bayou south of it; "The Burning" in Miss Theo's and Miss Myra's large house, Rose Hill, near Jackson, Mississippi, and briefly in Jackson itself; "Ladies in Spring" in a little Mississippi town called Royals; and "Kin" in a little "courthouse town, several hours by inconvenient train ride from Jackson." The remaining three stories are set far from the South: "The Bride of Innisfallen" on the boat train traveling from London to Cork; "Going to Naples" aboard the *Pomona* sailing from New York to Palermo and Naples; and "Circe" on her enchanted island. With the exception of "The Burning," all the stories have a decided comic strain, albeit in quite different ways. For example, in the melancholy "No Place for You, My Love," the woman's exasperating hat "was conspicuous, with some sort of glitter or flitter tied in a band around the straw and hanging down." It is such a prominent thing that the man, who has no interest in women's fashion and no eye for them himself, thinks the hat is wrong for her. Among the sights the nameless couple pass on their ride into the bayou is a Catholic church and its adjacent house. On the doorstep lies a "fresh-caught catfish the size of a baby—a fish wearing whiskers and bleeding," left perhaps by a parishioner or by the priest himself, who emerges from the house attired in most unpriestly garb—his underwear—to retrieve not only his fish but also his black gown, which has been airing on the clothesline, swaying "in a vague, trainlike, lady-like sweep." In spite of his undignified appearance, the priest stares at the car without a word, then collects the two incongruous items and disappears inside. He may have a catfish to attend to, but vespers are now at hand. Another humorous incongruity comes from the great contrast between eating establishments in the story. The nameless couple starts out in the elegance of Galatoire's, and their journey south takes them finally down an oyster-shell road to a beer shack called "Baba's Place." Printed menus are presented at Galatoire's, but at Baba's, an orange crayon sign, "Shrimp Dance Sun. PM," announces the menu and the entertainment.

In "The Bride of Innisfallen," the ship of fools setting in the boat-train compartment provides a medley of comic activities and people. The dominating figure is a woman, whose flowing raincoat of salmon-pink and yellow stripes and old blue hat settled on her head like an Indian bonnet make her stand out. A young passenger named Victor eats oranges and then chews the leather strap by the seat; a young schoolgirl reads and weeps over *Black Stallion of the Downs*, but stops long enough to eat a banana. It takes a Welshman three attempts to find his correct station and get off. When an English nurse carrying an Irish child pauses by the compartment door, the lady in the raincoat puffs on her cigarette and suggests they may be witnessing a kidnapping. Topics of conversation vary widely and are humorous in their presentation—the sound of Irish speech (especially when the audience is English); the death of a prized parrot; restrictions imposed by the Catholic Church; ghosts; and current horse race results. A greyhound named Telephone Girl, escaped temporarily from its owner, darts into the compartment and out again. Throughout these activities, the man from Connemara responds to everything with "*Oh* my God!" and all the passengers, except the American girl, eat and eat. The young schoolgirl has in her canvas satchel a "lunch box under lock and key, a banana, and a Bible." Victor consumes three oranges. Opening a paper parcel, the young wife offers everybody biscuits, declaring that she has oceans. As if to upstage such meager offerings, the lady in the raincoat "opened a parcel as big as a barrel and it was full of everything to eat that anybody could come out of England with alive": candy, jam roll, biscuits, bananas, nuts, sections of bursting orange, bread and butter, and several steaming thermoses of tea. They eat and talk as if engaged in a little party, and are hardly finished when their "hostess" puzzles everyone by announcing, "Well, *I'm* going to the sitting in the dining car now." (She had chicken, she tells them later.)

"Going to Naples" has its own peculiar passenger

list, starting with Gabriella Serto and her mother from
Buffalo. Part of the comedy arises from the stock situation of an anxious mother trying to get her daughter
paired off with an available young man. Certainly no
Daisy Miller, Gabriella, before land is out of sight, has
made it clear that whatever happens during the next two
weeks at sea, she has a scream for each moment and
every occasion. Matching Gabriella's screams are ear-
piercing "*Tweeeeets*" emitted by an old fellow on his ten-
cent whistle, who considers it his joke and his privilege to
alert "the whole assembly at life's most precious mo-
ments." As we have seen, Sister Anne in "Kin" has a
sadistic streak she is blind to, but at the same time she is
comic. Anxious for the visiting kin to meet the traveling
photographer, Mr. Alf J. Puryear ("there's some
Puryears in Mississippi"), she urges them to have their
pictures taken. "It's only a dollar down and you get them
in the *mail!*" Lavelle "Blackie" Coker ("Ladies in Spring")
plans a tryst in the woods with Opal Purcell which is
foiled in comic fashion. His son Dewey, who has spied
him from the school bus, "skimmed around the school
house door" to join him. Blackie is carrying two fishing
poles, adequate temptation for Dewey even though the
river is dry. A second foil to the meeting is Miss Hattie
Purcell, the local postmistress and self-appointed rain-
maker, who meets with success on this day and marches
all of them back into town—Blackie, Dewey, and her
niece Opal—beneath her large umbrella. Until the departure of Ulysses, leaving Circe with child and full of
grief, "Circe" is amusing in presenting the goddess's
fanatic domesticity and insistence on cleanliness from
travel-weary men about to be turned into swine.

Love, unfulfilled, thwarted, or lost, is a pervasive
theme in five of these seven stories. The man in "No
Place for You, My Love" had stayed in New Orleans an
extra day because his wife, at home in Syracuse, did not
want him there and underfoot with her guests, "some

old, unmarried college friends." When the woman asks
what his wife is like, the man says nothing, but merely
brings his right hand up and spreads it—"iron, wooden,
manicured." Whatever the relationship is, it has deterio-
rated beyond words. Early in the story, the man places
the woman's age at thirty-two and is quite sure she is
involved in a hopeless affair. After his severe reaction to
her question about his wife, "they did not risk going on
to her husband—if she had one." Someone, the woman's
husband or her lover, has given her a bruise above the
temple which she feels come out like an evil star. The
man's life in Syracuse and the woman's in Toledo are not
happy; furthermore, their day together in New Orleans
is not the beginning of a new life. The man kisses her,
"not knowing whether gently or harshly," and they part
with a handshake and no fulfillment of love. Their time
together has been governed in large part by the oppres-
sive July heat which bears down relentlessly. It is a de-
grading heat, the woman says, which sends New
Orleans natives home for naps, makes houses "hot as a
wall of growth," and turns the ferry into a hot stove.
With the heat have come swarms of insects, and the
combination creates discomfort and displeasure.

Gabriella's grandmother meets the *Pomona* in Naples and learns that Alpo Scampo has passionately
run after Gabriella during the trip. His attentions have
made her graceful on the dance floor in spite of her size,
and for a time even quelled her persistent screams. Whatever hope of happiness, whatever longing of Mrs. Serto
that Gabriella marry now at eighteen as her other daughters have done, are not to be realized through Aldo
Scampo, however. He leaves Gabriella with her mother
and grandmother and, laden with his two suitcases and
his cello, trudges into the big piazza to pursue cello study
in Rome under the G.I. bill.

Blackie is powerless, in "Ladies in Spring," to carry
out his plans with Opal. Dewey, his young son, does not

understand his fleeting glimpses of a woman in the woods calling his father's name, but he recognizes Miss Hattie Purcell's niece Opal, who steps out from among the elderberry bushes, plump as ever. Fifteen years later, Dewey realizes *she* was the woman who had called to his father that day in the woods.

The passengers in "The Bride of Innisfallen" illustrate varied examples of love. The woman in the raincoat has a man who carefully helps her on the train in London, and she is met in Cork by another man and several children. The pregnant woman in the "calm blue coat" is met in Cork by several people, but none of them appears to be her husband. The man from Connemara says women are jealous and uncertain creatures and thinks at times a certain person (presumably his wife) had something to do with the demise of his prize parrot. As critics have pointed out, the American girl has several counterparts in other Welty stories. Like Marjorie ("Flowers for Marjorie"), Hazel ("The Wide Net"), and Jinny Love Stark ("The Whole World Knows"), the American girl seems unable "to communicate to her husband some excess of joy which she therefore has to stifle to keep from getting out of hand."[14] In Cork she is released from the restrained behavior necessary with her husband and from her reticence among the strangers in the train compartment. Her spontaneous joy bursts out, conveyed through musical imagery of notes and arpeggios. "I see Cork's streets take off from the waterside and rise lifting their houses and towers like note above note on a page of music, with arpeggios running over it of green and galleries and belvederes, and the bright sun raining at the top. Out of joy I hide for fear it is promiscuous." Leaving her husband has brought her a full release and a sense of freedom, but the reader does not know if she ever returns to him. The telegram she starts twice is not sent to her husband but is dropped instead into the street as she turns toward the glad noises of the pub and takes her joy "into the lovely room full of strangers."

The cry of Circe as Ulysses's ship disappears across the waves is a cry of lost love and grief, compounded by her knowing how the story will end: Ulysses's son, whom she bears, will follow and slay him. Nothing relieves her grief, which "has no heavenly course; it is like mystery, and knows where to hide itself."

The Bride of Innisfallen remains a difficult volume, the stories complex, their meanings somewhat elusive, their style and subject matter radically different. "The Burning," Miss Welty's single Civil War story, embodies all the horrors of women left at home and unprotected during war. Rose Hill is invaded by Yankees on horseback, looted by them and by the slaves, and finally burned; the incredibly innocent Miss Myra is raped; she, her sister, and a servant, Delilah, walk to Jackson where Miss Theo directs Miss Myra's hanging and then her own; and a child of unexplained lineage is burned to death in the house. Moreover, the horrors come from every direction. Miss Theo callously suggests to the soldiers that they might satisfy themselves with one of the servants ("May I offer you this young kitchen Negro, as I've always understood—"), her precise and ladylike diction singularly at odds with her proposal. The intruding soldiers have no sense of value and destroy everything from the women's virtue to the peacocks, oblivious to the civilized order that perishes at their hands. Surrealistic scenes occur when Delilah returns to the burned house, peers into the Venetian mirror, and sees a vision, gathers up the bones of the dead child, the shoes and jewelry she had removed from the dead sisters, and placing all of it on her head, walks into the river, "stretching her throat like a sunflower stalk above the river's opaque skies."

Critics have commented on the influence of Elizabeth Bowen and Henry Green to explain Miss Welty's taste for ambiguity, the evasive hinting while withholding essential information, the circling around the point without revealing it.[15] In spite of its complexity and difficulties, *The Bride of Innisfallen* had some excellent re-

views. A few critics contend that her fiction is more successful when it is set on home ground, but few deny the
importance of *The Bride of Innisfallen* in the Welty canon.

Originally published as a short story in *The New
Yorker* (March 15, 1969), *The Optimist's Daughter* appeared
as a novel in 1972, and added to Miss Welty's already
numerous honors the Pulitzer Prize. A short novel, *The
Optimist's Daughter* is divided into four parts, the first
three of nearly equal length and the last quite brief. The
novel focuses on the eye surgery of Judge Clinton McKelva of Mount Salus, Mississippi; on his daughter, Laurel
McKelva Hand, who has come from her designer job in
Chicago to be with her father; and on his second wife,
Wanda Fay Chisom McKelva. Part one opens in New
Orleans during Mardi Gras, and against that carnival
atmosphere the characters keep a three-week hospital
vigil that ends in Judge McKelva's death. Part two begins
with the arrival of Laurel and Fay in Mount Salus with
the Judge's body, covers his funeral (an almost impossible
affair, with the neighbors' extravagant stories about the
judge as well as the Texas Chisoms' antic behavior), and
ends with Fay's sudden departure in the family pick-up
truck for a visit home. Parts three and four center on
Laurel's confrontation with the ghosts of the past and her
apparent success in accepting that "memory lived not in
initial possession but in the freed hands, pardoned and
freed and in the heart that can empty but fill again, in the
patterns restored by dreams." She can leave not only the
town but also her parents' house, her mother's roses (content in their memory, not needing their fragrance), and
especially her mother's breadboard, that symbol of
perfection and love which Laurel's husband Philip Hand
had made.

The New Orleans setting of part one introduces
major themes in the novel, particularly family relationships, loneliness, and the distress arising out of ill-

ness. Lines of social demarcation are also established which
place Dr. Courtland (who had grown up next door to the
McKelvas), Laurel, and the Judge in one camp; Fay and
the Dalzell family in another. Class distinctions occupy
much attention, as Fay's dress, talk, behavior, and values
continually clash with those upheld by the Mount Salus
community. Although much of this short novel is conveyed through dialogue and action, a great portion is also
told through Laurel, as she relives the past by examining
her father's desk and chair, the books in his library, her
mother's sewing room and her desk with the many
pigeonholes, where (unlike the Judge) she had saved all
remnants of the past. Structurally, one of the most skill-
ful parts of the novel is the opening chapter of part three,
where the four elderly neighbors—Miss Tennyson Bulloch (the major's wife and Tish's mother), Miss Adele
Courtland, Mrs. Bolt, and Mrs. Pease—discuss yet again
the puzzling question of how Judge McKelva, nearly
seventy, could have married a younger woman like Fay.
As they talk, Laurel silently works at her mother's flowers, not answering the four questions sent her way and
uttering only four short sentences in the entire chapter.
Almost like a musical interlude each voice of the gossipy
ladies strikes a different key and tempo, the recurrent
melodic refrain coming intermittently from the mocking
bird ("On top of the tree, the mockingbird threw out his
chest and let fall a cascade of song"). Laurel's virtual
silence, the fragrance of the roses, and the pure song of
the mockingbird, suggest the still center of this section
and indeed of the entire novel. The trappings of the
world are shut out, and Laurel retreats now into silence.
Later she faces the truth of the past and survives that
confrontation.

   Undergirding the structure of the novel is a persistent emphasis on time: if much time elapses before
surgery, Judge McKelva could lose all vision in his dam-
aged eye. Each morning he asks Laurel "What time her

watch showed?" a question Fay says a stranger could answer. The long hours of waiting, the enforced idleness, makes time hang heavy for them all. Forced to lie still, weighted with sandbags, warned not to cry, Judge McKelva must endure the tedious minutes, hours, and days of his convalescence. "What occupied his full mind was *time* itself; *time* passing: he was concentrating [italics added]." Dr. Courtland's daily remark is, "Nothing to do but give it more time," and to him the three weeks fly by; to patient and family, however, the time has been unending. To divert her father's attention, Laurel reads *Nicholas Nickleby*, which "seemed as endless to her as *time* must seem to him," and he apparently kept up with her page turning "with *time*, checking off moment after moment [italics added]." Fay cannot stand the pressure of waiting that the convalescence requires, and, driven by sounds of carnival noises and dancing, she lunges at the Judge, demanding his attention to her now. While Fay and Laurel stay in the waiting room until Dr. Courtland assesses what damage Fay has caused, Laurel looks at the clock on the wall, and when Dr. Courtland appears in the doorway to beckon them to the news of Judge McKelva's death, he stands with "the weight of his watch in his hand." After the body has been consigned to Mr. Pitts, the obsequious Mount Salus undertaker, and the neighbors finally leave the house to quiet, Laurel listens for "the striking of the mantel clock downstairs in the parlor. It never came." The clock was one her father always wound, having driven a nail (a little crookedly) for the key. When Laurel had first looked, the clock "pointed to some remote three o'clock" and stood "as motionless as the time in the Chinese prints" hung around it, brought by an earlier generation of McKelvas turned missionaries. Later, Laurel's friends (her six bridesmaids of years ago) wind the clock, and when she returns from the funeral, the time is "only ten minutes past noon." Twenty minutes later, Fay has decided to go with her family, and the clock strikes the half hour just at that moment. Fay cries, "Oh, how I hate that old striking clock! It's the first thing I'm going to get rid of."

For Laurel, time away from Chicago and her work has amounted to a month—three weeks in New Orleans, a week in Mount Salus—and she plans now to leave her father's house before Fay returns to assume full possession of it. Fay, however, comes early, in time for a confrontation with Laurel. In a kitchen cabinet Laurel has found the handmade breadboard, nicked and scarred from Fay's misuse and gnawed at by mice. Momentarily tempted to strike Fay with it, Laurel raises the board above her head; at that point, "from the parlor came a soft whirr, and noon struck." Immediately, Laurel lowers the board and her sensation of violence passes; she is summoned back to herself by the clock, by time, by reality. Complemented by this is an underlying concern with the past, which for Laurel holds memories of traditions and rituals, and for Fay, is nothing, the future everything. What Laurel learns to deal with is the present, to excise it from the past and live. The past is not obliterated for her, but it is relegated to memory which is not dependent on the physical presence of roses, breadboards, letters, recipes, school composition books, or the house of her youth.

Although it is a man who has died and thus brings all these events together, women dominate the novel. Four women have particular relationships to Judge McKelva. Becky Thurston, his first wife, retained an unending love for her West Virginia home. At last helpless from a stroke and blindness, Becky summoned and then humiliated the Presbyterian minister, responding to his remarks with only a cry of longing for home: "I'd like better than anything you can tell me just to see the mountain one more time." Alive, Becky had been independent and self-sufficient, Laurel thinks, as she turns to a photograph in the album. The red blouse

Becky wore in the picture was the most prized garment
she ever had. The cloth was made from thread spun by
her mother's own hand; the deep, rich, American-
beauty-red color was created from pokeberries. Becky
had made the blouse, and probably developed the pictures Laurel is looking at, and "very likely she had made
the paste that held them." Her strong character pushes
her he had died of a ruptured appendix. Her last remark to
marry a coward, she asks of Judge McKelva. When in
despair over her condition he promises to take her back to
her mountains, she calls him "Lucifer! Liar!" In her
youth, Becky had performed incredible tasks, the most
significant an icy winter trip on a raft bearing her sick
father to Baltimore, where she stood alone as doctors told
her he had died of a ruptured appendix. Her last remark
to Laurel painfully indicates the shortcomings that she
sees in her daughter. "You could have saved your mother's
life. But you stood by and wouldn't intervene. I despair
for you."

Whatever tender memories Laurel holds about her
mother are matched by recollections not so dear. When
the Judge arranged for pink champagne from New
Orleans and a five-piece black band for Laurel's wartime
wedding, Becky called his expenses utter extravagance,
childfoolishness. As Mayor and later as Judge, Laurel's
father was necessarily cast into the public eye, but Becky
"would rather go through anything than a grand occasion." She was more interested in mulching her flowers
than in dressing stylishly. When the Judge bought her a
dress of beaded crepe, she retorted, "Clinton, if I'd been
told in advance you were going to make me an extravagant present, I'd have asked you for a load of floor sweep-
ings from the cottonseed-mill." Her bread baking, her
reading aloud at night with Clinton, her efficient courage
as a child, her fighting for life, were not sufficient in the
end to bring her or her family comfort. "She had died
without speaking a word, keeping everything to herself,

in exile and humiliation." Of herself and of others she had demanded too much, and in the end, she could neither give nor receive comfort.

Fay is seemingly Becky's opposite. The only kitchen implement she knows by name is a frying pan, she does not know how to separate an egg, and she could not imagine why Becky had gone to the trouble of making bread since it all tastes the same anyway. Pruning roses never occurs to her, fine old furniture means nothing— she has trailed drops of red nail polish on the Judge's desk and transformed the mahogany headboard of the bed into a sea of quilted peach satin. She cracks walnuts on the breadboard, lets mice run unchecked in the kitchen, leaves the bed unmade when they go to New Orleans, and protests to the doctor that nature is the best healer for her husband's slipped retina. Unlike Becky, whose family were lawyers and teachers and bank officials, Fay's brother Bubba operates a wrecking concern and DeWitt has a front yard littered with appliances he has never gotten around to repairing. Becky's love of books is foreign to Fay, who has complete disregard for reading. She had told the Judge that "if he hadn't spent so many years of his life poring over dusty old books, his eyes would have more strength saved up for now." Whatever terms of endearment Becky spoke in the blossoming of romance and married life, "*Hon*," Fay's familiar expression, was not among them. She is what Becky had feared and predicted for the Judge. Lacking Becky's courage, Fay whines throughout the Judge's hospital stay that she had planned to dance and shop in New Orleans, not nurse the sick; when the Judge dies, she screams: "You picked my birthday to do it on!" Fay may be common, but she has caught and pleased the Judge nevertheless, and tried, she protests to Laurel, to be a wife to him. As Missouri, the black cook testifies, Fay gave the Judge the pleasure of spoiling her.

Hints in the novel suggest that the Judge's next-

door neighbor, Adele Courtland, might have been a willing and, by Mount Salus standards, a most suitable
second wife. A spinster school teacher, Miss Adele is
kind, efficient, and candid. She helps Laurel keep some
perspective about the past, puts the McKelva kitchen to
order after the funeral crowds, and reminds the neighbors that the boisterous Chisoms are only "a trifle more
inelegant" than Mount Salus citizens at the Judge's funeral. Her refined and gentle manner, however, has another
side, although not always apparent—the faint note of
mockery in her voice. Like the other neighbors, she totally misjudges Laurel, agreeing that she should stay in
Mount Salus rather than return to Chicago. "Laurel,"
she declares quite incorrectly, "has no other life." The
mockery in her voice gets stronger when she remarks that
her brother Nate's adorable French wife Betty in New
Orleans "would agree with Laurel perfectly: there's not
enough Mount Salus has to *offer* a brilliant mind." Miss
Adele continues, insisting that Laurel can do anything if
it is made hard enough for her. "Of *course* she can give up
Mount Salus, and say goodbye to this house and to us,
and the past, and go back to Chicago day after tomorrow,
flying a jet. And take up one more time where she left
off." Laurel, however, recognizing Miss Adele's mockery, "stood up and kissed the mischievous, wrinkled
cheek." Apparently more gentle than Becky, and pos-
sessed of those qualities the town admires, Miss
Adele would have been the ideal second wife. Yet as
Laurel watches out the kitchen window, she sees Miss
Adele turn from the clothesline to wave at her: "She
beckons with her pain, thought Laurel, realizing how
often her father must have stood just here, resting his
eyes, and looked out at her without even seeing her."
If the perfect second wife did live right next door,
Judge McKelva never realized it.

    Laurel, of course, is the fourth woman. Helpless in
his illness, the Judge never asks Laurel how she can be

away from her work. He "left his questions unasked. But both knew, and for the same reason, that bad days go better without any questions at all." Laurel, not Fay, asks the doctor the responsible questions and acts as the stabilizing influence. Her own life had been blessed and then shattered in marriage. Her young architect husband died in World War II on board a Navy ship; but before his death their brief marriage was one of magical ease, not subjected to the problems her parents faced through time and illness. Now Laurel is independent and alone, no longer a part of the Mount Salus she had known. Her years away have postponed the examination of the past which her father's death now necessitates. Alone, Laurel experiences a difficult time; her troubled spirit, only hinted at early in the novel, now demands attention. As Cleanth Brooks points out, the sooty chimney swift that darts in the house soils the freshly washed curtains the way Fay's presence ruins objects and memories dear to Laurel. That trapped bird, frantic but powerless to escape, is Laurel, "trapped in the past that is suddenly strange and problematical."[16] The terrors of the bird and of Laurel coalesce. When morning comes, neither the miserable Mr. Cheek nor Missouri can get the bird out, so Laurel herself traps it in two straw baskets and releases it to the wind declaring, "I'll *make* it go free." As the bird disappears to nothing more than "a tilting crescent being drawn into the sky," Missouri says, "All birds got to fly, even them no-count dirty ones," and returns to rewash the curtains. Like the chimney swift, Laurel *makes* herself go free, disallowing, but not forgetting, the past.

In addition to these prominent characters are some half-dozen eccentric, almost vulgar, minor ones from Mount Salus. Major Rupert Bullock, lifelong friend of the Judge, is tipsy and speaks like a Chisom to Fay as she stands over the coffin. "Just tell him goodbye, Sugar. . . . That's best, just plant him a kiss." Among the funeral callers is Dot Daggart, the Judge's private secretary for years, who was furious over his retirement even though he had gotten her another job. Her age and physical characteristics make an amusing incongruity. About seventy, Dot approaches the coffin "with her nonchalant, twenties stalk on her high heels," and says in her throaty baritone, "I couldn't resist." She takes offense at a perfectly innocent remark Miss Tennyson Bullock makes, and sticks by her resolve never to speak to Tennyson again. At the funeral, she plays the part of the grand lady, announcing to Laurel that she has seen everybody in Mount Salus she used to know. Her exit is worthy of the cinema: "Dot looked up at Laurel out of her old movie-actress eyes. Kissing her hand to the others, she told them goodbye, cutting Miss Tennyson Bulloch."

Other eccentrics include Verna Longmeier, the sewing woman, a big, apple-cheeked woman with a hairy tam for a hat, and shoes rundown at the heels. In the past, she had spent days sewing for people, never acknowledging that she made crooked seams and always twisting the stories she told. She lumbered toward Laurel announcing to all within hearing another twisted story: "'I remember, oh, I remember how many Christmases I was among those present in this dear old home in all its hospitality. . . . And they'd throw open those doors between these double parlors and the music would strike up; and then'—Miss Verna drew out her arm as though to measure a yard—'then Clinton and I, we'd lead out the dance.'" There were, of course, no such Christmas dances. Mrs. Pease, a neighbor whose solitariness is symbolized by her untresspassed garden, stations herself behind the draperies in the McKelva home and watches people come up the walk. When she appears after the funeral, she is working crablike on a huge afghan. The worst of these people is Mr. Cheek, a perennial jack-leg carpenter. Officious, suggestive, insolent, and inefficient, he cannot expel the chimney swift, as he claimed, but does tramp over the house, thoroughly exasperating Laurel. As he opens the big bedroom door, the bird flies in. "'That's about my favorite room in the house,' he said. He gave Laurel a black grin; his front teeth had gone." Since Laurel has not yet "married another somebody," Mr. Cheek suggests that perhaps they ought to get together. He has gossiped with Fay about Becky, and all in all succeeds in being offensive physically and verbally. The presence of these characters makes Mount Salus more complete, their brief appearance sufficient to convey a full sense of the community. Furthermore, they balance the boisterous Chisoms and Dalzells, also comic and vulgar.

The Optimist's Daughter shares with other of Miss Welty's works a thematic interest in family, community, social mores, marriage, loneliness, and the continuity of life that love provides. In addition, considerable attention is devoted to the trial of illness and the imposition of hospital routine upon life. The first part of the novel explores the helpless dependency that illness can cause— Judge McKelva must admit that something is wrong which he is powerless to correct. He waives a second opinion, considering himself in good hands because he knows Nate Courtland. Fay distrusts Dr. Courtland and, scoffing at his manners, declares, "I bet when the bill comes in he won't charge as polite." The entire Chisom clan distrusts the motives and actions of doctors and nurses. Mrs. Chisom attributes the Judge's death to his electing to enter the hospital. Bubba's philosophy is short and simple—"Doctors don't know what they're doing. They just know how to charge." Sis assures everybody within earshot that "what they let go on in hospitals don't hardly bear repeating," and quotes Irma who said that what happens in the maternity ward in Amarillo "would curl your hair." Doctors overcharge, and nurses are culpable—Mrs. Chisom would not trust one behind her back for a blessed second. The Chisoms' remarks are cliches, but the actual behavior of Dr. Courtland and the various nurses is less than ideal. The night nurse, Mrs. Martello, divides her attention between Judge McKelva and her crocheting—she has finished twenty-seven pairs of bootees. "'You'd be surprised how fast I give out of 'em,' she said. 'It's the most popular present there is.'" Her incorrect grammar and her uncalled-for familiarities do not alter her tone of authority as she warns Fay not to jostle the Judge. "The nurse, without stopping her crochet hook, spoke from the chair. 'Don't go near that eye, hon! Don't nobody touch him or monkey with that eye of his, and don't even touch the bed he's on, till Dr. Courtland says touch, or somebody'll be mighty sorry. And Dr. Courtland will skin me alive.'"

While Dr. Courtland is solicitous toward the Judge and Laurel, he pays little attention to Fay's outbursts, having seen her kind many times before. The success of the operation elates him "as though he had just come from a party." Laurel's daily problem is catching him on his lightning-quick visits and dealing with his explanations. Three weeks is not long enough to ensure the healing needed, and when Laurel asks if the drugs are responsible for her father's seeming to be unlike himself and at so great a distance, the doctor's answer is indirect and useless. "Well, no two people react in the same way to everything. . . . People are different, Laurel."

After Fay's sudden attack on the Judge, Mrs. Martello struggles with her, panting as she speaks to Laurel, her true self emerging in her appearance, speech, and protective attitude. Her basic instinct may be right, but her manners and actions are common and insensitive, her nurse's image a shell.

"She laid hands on him! She said if he didn't snap out of it, she'd—" The veneer of nurse slipped from Mrs. Martello—she pushed up at Laurel the red, shocked face of a Mississippi countrywoman as her voice rose to a clear singsong. "She taken ahold of him. She was abusing him." The word went echoing. "I think she was fixing to pull him out of that bed." . . . Mrs. Martello added wildly, "*She's* not a nurse!" She swung her starched body around and sent her voice back toward Judge McKelva's door. "What's the matter with that woman? Does she want to *ruin* your eye?"

Summoned, Dr. Courtland appears in his evening clothes, sends Fay and Laurel to the waiting room, and turns to look at a dead Judge McKelva. Both nurse and doctor speak as if in dying the patient has played a sly trick on the medical world. "'Now what did *he* pull?' Mrs. Martello cried." Laurel is still in earshot for the doctor's answer. "The renegade! I believe he's just plain sneaked out on us." Cheated of ever knowing the full effect of his operation on the Judge, Dr. Courtland later looks protestingly at the lighted elevator numbers flashing by and says, "I'd been waiting to know how well that eye would *see!*" Fay's parting remarks to Dr. Courtland as she is driven from the hospital emphasize the lack of rationale she always exhibits, as well as the frustration survivors and doctors share. "'All I hope is *you* lay awake tonight and remember how little you were good for. . . . Thank you for nothing!' Fay screamed above the whir of their riding away."

As John Desmond has pointed out, "the family as both vital center and/or threatening enclosure which stifles itself,"[17] is the dominant theme in *Delta Wedding*, *The Golden Apples*, and *Losing Battles*, and certainly one can include *The Optimist's Daughter* in the list. The McKelva family—Clinton, Becky, and Laurel—were bound together by tradition, social position, values. Flower gardens were maintained, social occasions observed, civic responsibilities carried out. Their private selves, however, present all three as decidedly lonely individuals, dependent at last only on their own strength, not on the family unit. The nuclear family here dissolves, but the entire way of community life in Mount Salus has also seriously eroded. Laurel's bridesmaids all live in new suburban houses, her friend Tish has a fifteen-year-old son she does not understand (girls climb in his bedroom window to play chess, he says), the cemetery overlooks the highway, and the McKelva homeplace now belongs to a Chisom from Texas. When Miss Tennyson Bullock urges Laurel to forget about drawing all those pictures in Chicago, she foolishly offers a prospect of the past. "As I was saying to Tish, 'Tish, if Laurel would stay home and Adele would retire, we could have as tough a bridge foursome as we had when Becky was playing.'" The past, however, will not be repeated. Miss Tennyson's proposal, Judge McKelva's grotesque funeral, and Laurel's night of facing the past are just three among many signals that time has wrought inevitable changes. Miss Welty's *The Optimist's Daughter* does indeed have "the power and authority of a small masterpiece. Line by line, her writing has never been better."[18]

5

^^^^^^^^^^^^^^^^^^^^^^^^^

The High Art
of Eudora Welty

The March 21, 1943 issue of *The New York Times Book Review* carried an article by Orville Prescott entitled "A Handful of Rising Stars." Although many of the ten authors Prescott mentioned in the article are forgotten today, he wisely recognized Miss Welty's talent, calling her "a distinguished artist, something of a poet, an ironic, savage observer of the human comedy."[1] Since that time, that rising star has become prominently fixed in the skies. Imagination and passion remain the heart of Miss Welty's writing principle and are complemented by a practical and methodical process of composition. Although she can write anywhere, Miss Welty prefers to write at home—the most convenient place for the early riser that she is. The ideal situation, she says, is to write the whole first draft in one sitting, to work on revisions as long as needed, and then to write the final version all in one sitting—a long, sustained effort. She revises with scissors and pins placing pieces of typed manuscript on the rug, the bed, or the dining-room table (as someone might do who sews at home, she has explained), and then her objective eye can decide how a transposition will or will not work. This revising is a process Miss Welty loves doing—"putting things in their best and proper place," recognizing the kernel of the story and knowing instinctively not to touch something if it is right.[2] Despite a high regard for Faulkner, Miss Welty has never been within his shadow as a writer, and she has always been completely capable of pursuing her goals and aims without any dependence or attachment. Recently, looking back at her first story, "Death of a Traveling Salesman," she remarked that it has remained "a member of the general family of my work, not lacking in earmarks good and bad. I find it still packs a challenge for its author, for which I respect it."[3] All her work commands respect from her readers, and it in turn has given them delight and wisdom, understanding and insight, feelings of compassion and love.

The South of the twentieth century has undergone major changes and, as Louis Rubin contends, has provided a culture more conducive to writers than many other geographic sections.[4] From 1910 to 1960, for example, many middle western writers called for social reforms and went east, many eastern writers fled to Paris and Rome to purify their art form, and most southern writers—including Eudora Welty—stayed home and sought to correct rather than destroy their heritage.[5]

Although her travels have taken her across the United States and to Europe, Miss Welty has indeed remained at home—not just in the South, but in the same place in the South, Jackson, Mississippi. Except for a handful, her stories are set in the South, most often in Mississippi where her towns of Clay, Polk, Beulah, Royals, Banner, Cane Springs, Morgana, Yellow Leaf, China Grove, Natchez, Victory, Dover, Ellisville, and Dexter are concrete locales from which fascinating characters emerge singing, working, eating, playing, pondering, and, above all else, talking.[6] Like the names of the towns the characters' names are carefully chosen, and by their very being often suggest a trait of personality, a family connection, or a fanciful indulgence. Leota, Thelma, Mrs. Pike, and Mrs. Fletcher are names as sharp and biting as the characters themselves. In *The Ponder Heart*, Edna Earle's name suggests not only the virtuous and indomitable heroine of the domestic sentimental novel *St. Elmo*, but also the southern habit of giving double names, which we also see in Stella-Rondo and Shirley-T., Billy Boy, Wanda Fay, William Wallace, Robbie Bell, Jinny Love, Bonnie Dee, Jim Allen, and Maude Eva. (Another Edna Earle, in "The Wide Net," is to this day probably still wondering how "the little tail of the 'C' got through the 'L' in a Coca-Cola sign.") Occasionally, characters have exotic names—Gypsy, Powerhouse, Uranus Knockwood, India—that make them partly alien to the familiar southern surroundings. Others have names that hint of intriguing origins—Mr. Bobo, Miss Billy Texas Spights, Miss Teacake Magee, Mr. Truex Bodkin, and Ears Broadwee. Aunt Birdie's real name is even more unusual than the one she goes by (*Losing Battles*). Named Virgil Homer after two doctors, she was called both names. "It wasn't till I tried saying it myself and it came out 'Birdie' that I ever got it any different." The foundling, Gloria Short, was named by the Home Demonstration Agent: "It was a glorious day and she was sorry she had to cut her visit so short, Gloria Short." Some characters' names reflect a physical detail or their position in the family. Thus, sons may bear their father's given name, but with "Little" preceding it. (In *Delta Wedding*, one son is called "Little Battle.") Sister, Sis, Bubba, and Granny are names that establish family relationships, while Old Phoenix, Old Lethy, Old Man Moody, and Old Man Fate Rainey indicate the characters' age. The southern habit of titles is quite pervasive, with "Miss" preceding the given names of married women—Miss Tennyson (Mrs. Rupert Bulloch), Miss Beulah (Mrs. Ralph Renfro), Miss Lizzie Stark (Mrs. Comus Stark), Miss Katie (Mrs. Fate Rainey)—and unmarried women—Miss Theo, Miss Myra, Miss Lexie, Miss Adele. A few male characters always have "Mr." preceding their names—Mr. Gene, Mr. Whitaker (we are never told his given name), Mr. Fatty Bowles. Country Baptist preachers are often called "Brother" (Brother Bethune), and *Major* Bulloch retains his military title but with no explanation of its history. A few characters bear extremely formal names—Octavia, Gerald, Phoebe, Lotte Elisabeth Eckhart—and names of blacks are characteristically colorful and evocative: Exum, Twosie, Plez, Phoenix, Narciss, Missouri.

Many characters' names were changed when stories were revised. Miss Welty explained why the name "Rafe" in the 1936 publication of "Death of a Traveling Salesman" became "Sonny" when that story appeared in the collection, *A Curtain of Green* (1941):

I had got sensitive to the importance of proper names, and this change is justified: "Sonny" is omnipresent in boys' names in Mississippi and is not dropped just because boys grow up and marry; "Sonny" helped make the relationship of the man and woman one that Bowman could mistake at the beginning; and at the same time it harked back to the fire-bringer.[7]

Not every revised name brought so many excellent results, but given names, surnames, nicknames, titles, and descriptive epithets are a significant part of the flavor of Miss Welty's fiction. The names are characteristically southern, and when they are not—Miss Lotte Elisabeth Eckhart, for example—the character is instantly recognized as an outsider.

Miss Welty has certainly embraced the traditional southern temper—a sense of the concrete, the elemental, and the ornamental, a fascination with the folk tale or story "told and retold, filled out by hazard and by guess, in the long afternoons and evenings of the Southern home, store, or public square."[8] The South perhaps more than any other region in the country distinguishes *place* from *scene* (individualized space), because place to the southerner is fixed, "but also associated with neighboring spaces that share a history, some communicable tradition and idiom, according to which a personality can be identified."[9] In her essay "Place in Fiction," Miss Welty wrote that "*feelings are bound up in place.*" It may be "one of the lesser angels that watch over the racing hand of fiction," but, "the moment the place in which the novel happens is accepted as true, through it will begin to glow, in a kind of recognized glory, the feeling and thought that inhabited the novel in the author's head and animated the whole of his work." In Miss Welty's fiction, place includes the town and its families, further back in generations and family history than one can imagine; characters with names, habits, and voices that are unerringly true; field crops, flowers, heirlooms, house furnishings that exist in an atmosphere of hot weather and cold, late frosts and droughts, summer thunder showers and equinoctial storms. "The minutiae of place are vividly clear and precise, even at the moment of their dying, because of the promise of and the provision for their imaginative renewal."[10]

As many critics have pointed out, with few exceptions Miss Welty has not found the South's defeat in the Civil War, the collective guilt over slavery, the insistent agrarian role, or the rise and fall of social ranks aspects of southern history to shape into fiction. "Human life is fiction's only theme," she has declared. A first generation southerner, Miss Welty knows her South well and has long since stopped being irked by the label *regional*. "I just think of myself as writing about human beings and I happen to live in a region, as do we all, so I write about what I know—it's the same case for any writer living anywhere. I also happen to love my particular region. If this shows, I don't mind."[11] When Miss Welty talks with interviewers, one subject that always gets much attention is the natural proclivity of the southerner to be a talker, and a talker accustomed to an audience. That talking gift of the southern female, Robert Penn Warren has recently noted, is almost lost in the temper of time. "I now hear it in no one younger than 50—and rarely that young—nor the imagination, sensibility, wit, humor, mimicry and pity that usually go with it."[12] To an extent, Warren is right, for new modes of entertainment have, even in the South, been strong rivals to tale telling and talk. Nevertheless, even among women and men younger than fifty, there are still tales told and retold, there is still deference given—Let Julia tell that one. She gets it just right.—to some more skilled talker, and there are still late nights on porch and by fireside when stories are retold and tales are swapped, even if the number of talkers has been sharply reduced by competition from television sets and electronic games.

The South in most of Miss Welty's fiction is rural or small town, a South relatively unconcerned with delicatessens and apartment complexes, housing projects and rapid transit. It is a South of much talk, which gives a great sense about people's lives. "You know several generations because they all live together. You know what happened to So-and-so clear through his life. You get a narrative sense of your next door neighbor instead of someone you just met in the supermarket, which you do today, or you just see people in flashes."[13] Large cities like New York, Miss Welty has said, can bring you the greatest and most congenial friends, "but it's extraordinary if you ever know anything about them except that little wedge of their life that you meet with the little wedge of your life."[14] Although Elizabeth Bowen expressed delight in having Miss Welty as a houseguest, it was not a *southern* meeting or setting: "I really know little about her life, nor she about mine." The characteristic is quite clear in Miss Welty's fiction when an outsider like Miss Eckhart ("June Recital") appears. We never learn where she and her mother came from or why they left, why they came to Morgana, or what the men in their family did for a living. If they have tales of delight or sorrow to tell, we never hear them. Their habit of conversation is reduced to brief questions and answers and sparse comments. Miss Eckhart and her mother w[e] never, like the Chisoms and the Dalzells, join in vy[?] and trouble swapping; a family reunion is the remotest c[?]. social activities to them; they would never, even if invited, sit on the porch and talk a summer's evening away. The habit of talk for southerners is a source of knowledge and entertainment; it encourages, Miss Welty says, "exaggeration and the comic . . . because tales get taller as they go along. But I think beneath all of that is a sense, really, of caring about one another. It is a pleasure and an entertainment, but it's also of deep significance to people."[15]

Miss Welty's South has been a fruitful source for her work. Seeing an old black woman walk against the horizon, clearly bent on a mission, and hearing another one say "I too old at the surrender," were starting points for "A Worn Path"; a tale told at a WPA fair became the central issue in "Keela, the Outcast Indian Maiden," an episode that had to be true since it was too outrageous to have been made up. Indeed, the Old Natchez Trace, the 200 miles through the wilderness between Natchez and Nashville, was the trail of so many kinds of people and of so much activity, that to write of it, Miss Welty has said, "is enough to keep you busy for life."

It is impossible to think of southern fiction of the past forty-five years without seeing Eudora Welty. Although throughout her career she has written with a moral consciousness about her vision of life, the virtual absence of racial confrontations and issues in her fiction has brought sharp criticism. In the 1960s, late-night telephone calls from anonymous voices demanding, "Why don't you write stories about racial injustice?", forced Miss Welty to secure an unlisted telephone number. The complaints over social issues, however, began even earlier. In January 1940, James Laughlin of *New Directions* rejected "Keela, the Outcast Indian Maiden" because he foresaw three objections: some would say it derived too

much from Erskine Caldwell; it was not a "new direction"; and it would not enhance the South in the eyes of
the North. New York critics complained that *Delta Wedding* (1946) failed to recognize and confront "the moral
and sociological shortcomings of life in the Mississippi
Delta."[16] Margaret Marshall reviewed *The Golden Apples*
(1949) in the September 10, 1949, issue of *The Nation* and
charged that the "reader is scarcely ever made aware of
the mixed racial background which must surely affect the
quality of life even in the main families of small towns in
the deep South."[17] It is true that the changing race rela-
tion is not an issue met head-on in many of Miss Welty's
stories or novels, although several stories focus on black
characters ("A Worn Path," "Keela, the Outcast Indian
Maiden," "Powerhouse," and "Livvie").

In her reflections on the past, Laurel of *The Optimist's Daughter* says, "What burdens we lay on the dying."
The sentence can be aptly transposed: "What burdens
we lay on the writer," some readers and critics presum-
ing to dictate subject matter and political stances.
Addressing this problem, Walter Sullivan contends that
"if one disregards such books as *Absalom, Absalom!*,
which was written in the thirties and which is, properly
speaking, about innocence and pride, I know of no contemporary novel about the race problem which is likely
to survive. Yet, whatever his own views, the writer is
badgered by critics and public to speak to the issues."[18]
Miss Welty has, of course, faced the issue in an essay,
"Must the Novelist Crusade?" where she observes that
because the artist's imagination cannot say NO, he or she
is blocked from being a crusader. The voice of the crusader uses words not as words but as noisemakers, and,
brandishing them threatens, brags, or condemns. An
artist like Miss Welty must withdraw from such a public
arena. "Fiction," she wrote, "has, and must keep a private address. For life is *lived* in a private place; where it
means anything is inside the mind and heart." Her
answer to those who continue to ask why she has not

written stories about human injustice is eloquent and instructive:

> Well, I think I've always written stories about that. Not as propaganda, but I've written stories about human injustice as much as I've ever written about anything. It was not new to me that people were being unjust to one another then, because I had written about that in all of my work, along with other things people have been. I was looking at it in the human, not the political vision, and I was sticking to that. I didn't want to be swerved into preaching disguised as a work of fiction. . . . All great, great works have been moral documents in their way, too. And it's nothing new.[19]

Her black characters are not in the midst of making a cultural transition into the white world of academics, society, or business. They remain black, but their essential humanity is clearly in evidence in their relationship with nature, their unfailing devotion to family, their manner of living. Although not a prominent element in her fiction, Miss Welty's "treatment of Negroes defies almost any definable stock responses."[20] Furthermore, a close study of Miss Welty's photographs shows her deep understanding of these characters, ranging from Keela or Little Lee Roy, the club-footed black exploited by the sideshow and faintly reminiscent of African mythology, to a sophisticated jazz musician, to Phoenix Jackson, who embodies the word "charity," a virtue totally missing in the white people she encounters.[21] The hunter, the lady who ties her shoes, and the doctor's nurse all do something for Phoenix, but none of these chance benefactors perceive what Phoenix is—one who undertakes the arduous journey without question or complaint and undertakes it simply out of love. She is, to the minds of many readers, a saint, "one of those who walks always in the eye of God."[22] Rachael in "Kin," Narciss in *The Ponder Heart*, Roxie in *Delta Wedding*, and Missouri in *The Optimist's Daughter*, all are servants and do not play major roles; nevertheless, they are a vital part of the household.

135

.h could make Missouri come to the
to cook on Súnday (one can picture Mis-
.ting in the "Pageant of Birds" Miss Welty
d and wrote about), but she alone is for
minder of happier days. It is to Missouri's
g arms that Laurel turns twice in the novel.
Repo. rial details about numerous black characters are
given, and the scenes are brief vignettes with no authorial
comment. It is the scene itself that must strike readers
and show them the humor or the pathos, the ridiculous-
ness or the tragedy.

In "Why I Live at the P.O.," Sister relates her
mama's stereotyped view about black help on holidays.
"Mama had turned both the niggers loose: she always
said no earthly power could hold one anyway on the
Fourth of July, so she wouldn't even try. It turned out
that Jaypan fell in the lake and came within a very narrow limit of drowning." When Sister moves all her possessions to the post office, where she intends to live, a
little black girl makes nine trips from house to post office
with her Express wagon, hauling everything from Sister's wall calendar to the sewing machine motor. The
payment she receives comes from Uncle Rondo, whose
conduct in comparison with anyone else's is poor. "Uncle
Rondo came out on the porch and threw her a nickel."
Old Lethy, Mr. Farr's nurse so many years ago and so
close to him before the family in "Clytie" began its descent into madness, is treated heartlessly. After Mr. Farr
is bedridden, he and Old Lethy plead to see each other,
but Octavia refuses by shouting as she always has, and
Old Lethy is sent away as if she were an intruder. When
she hears that Mr. Farr is dying, she tries again, only to
be ordered away. Jamey in "A Curtain of Green" is the
docile and hard-working garden helper who is almost
killed by Mrs. Larkin in her siege of helpless fury. Old
Plez Morgan in "Shower of Gold" does not tell Snowdie
MacLain that the man on her porch was her husband

King, for fear that the news and King's immediate departure will hurt her. Plez, Miss Katie Rainey explains, is
the "real old kind, that knows everybody since time was."
The black characters in Miss Welty's fiction are not presented in roles of active social protest, but they generally
dignify the lives they live. The reader surely sees Mama's
narrow-minded view and Uncle Rondo's gratuitous gesture as evidence of human injustice, a condition Miss
Welty has always responded to.

Miss Welty published only two stories in the 1960s,
and both—"Where Is the Voice Coming From?" (1963)
and "The Demonstrators" (1966)—did center on contemporary social difficulties. The murder of Medgar Evers
on June 12, 1963, in Jackson, Mississippi, shocked the
nation. Miss Welty's reaction was voiced in "Where Is
the Voice Coming From?" At least four other titles for
the story were considered: "From the Unknown," "A
Voice from a Jackson Interior," "It Ain't Even July Yet,"
and "Voice from an Unknown Interior."[23] The earliest
version had actual names of Jackson people, streets,
businesses, and landmarks, all of which were transposed
to fictional counterparts. Miss Welty's discerning analysis of the entire tragedy was quite astute, but in pinpoint-
ing the social background of the murderer she was a little
wide of the mark. As a friend noted: "You thought it was
a Snopes and it was a Compson."[24] An interesting reaction to the story came from Flannery O'Connor, whose
friend Ashley Brown had sent her a copy. She wrote her
thanks on August 13, 1963, and added: "Nobody else
could have got away with it or made it work but her I
think. I want to read it again."[25] Some two and a half
weeks later, Miss O'Connor wrote to her friend "A" and
again mentioned "Where Is the Voice Coming From?",
this time after a second reading.

You are right about the Welty story. It's the kind of story that
the more you think about it the less satisfactory it gets. What I

hate most is its being the *New Yorker* and all the stupid Yankee liberals smacking their lips over typical life in the dear old dirty Southland. The topical is poison. I got away with it in "Everything That Rises Must Converge" but only because I say a plague on everybody's house as far as the race business goes.[26]

Certainly, neither Miss O'Connor nor Miss Welty can be accused of insensitivity to human need or trouble, and, certainly, no two southern writers have ever written with a higher sense of moral consciousness. To the serious and thoughtful artist, the topical is poison, demanding quick words and reflex responses. The question of a contemporary setting for a contemporary problem is not really the point; basic problems are *always* contemporary.[27]

As Ruth M. Vande Kieft has pointed out, the mystery and changes of human personality and relationships, the great themes in Miss Welty's fiction, are of the inner life, and for the characters it is feelings, not words, that prevail. The young American girl in "The Bride of Innisfallen" cannot even find the words for a telegram to her husband, yet the change in their relationship is all important, if unexpressed. To Miss Welty, the mechanics of a story—getting people in and out of rooms, putting on clothes, performing an action like sewing that she herself does not do well—are the hardest things in writing; the easiest things for her to write about are the emotions, and so often the emotions of the inner life.[28] Loneliness, primal joy, the impulse that prompts celebration, the power present in the continuity of love, the forming and the dissolving of family isolation, private sensibility, the mystery of human life itself, are states of being that Miss Welty's characters face. In husband-wife relationships, different inner responses to life cause problems that lead to misunderstanding and sometimes separation (physical or spiritual): for example, Howard and Marjorie, William Wallace and Hazel, Robbie and George, the American girl and her husband, the respective spouses of the man and woman in "No Place for You, My Love," Jack

and Gloria Renfro, Judge McKelva and Becky. To be
sure, the degrees of misunderstanding vary and the res-
olutions are by no means the same. Howard and Marjorie's dilemma ends tragically; William Wallace and
Hazel are reconciled, at least for the moment, as are
Robbie and George. Just what resolution the American
girl and her husband will find we are not told, and we do
not definitely see Jack and Gloria Renfro settle their differences—Jack wants *all* his family to remain together,
while Gloria struggles for the independence of her marriage unit. Judge McKelva at the end cannot comfort his
wife Becky with word or deed.

Certainly in Miss Welty's very first story, R. J.
Bowman, that lonely and sick traveling salesman, sees
and envies the simple but fruitful marriage that Sonny
and his woman enjoy. For Bowman, there is nothing but
loneliness and isolation, exclusion from a family circle,
and for him there comes no compensating primal joy,
only a lonely death. The family, however, is not an im-
pervious stronghold, resistant to change, but "a double-
edged weapon. Its conservatism and protectionism stifles
as well as shelters."[29] From Sister who leaves home in a
huff, to India and Dabney Fairchild whose actions signal
significant family adjustments, to Laurel who did not
stay at home and look after her widowed father, to the
various unhappy marriages in *The Golden Apples*, to Fay
who denies that she even has any living family, examples
abound which show that however strong and happy the
family appears to be, time and circumstance can and
usually will bring disruptive changes. This is not to
minimize the frequent happy celebrations of family life
that also come in Miss Welty's fiction. Nevertheless, that
neither the family nor the individual is invulnerable
underscores the risks her characters must face and the
inevitable changes they must undergo. Those who find
love and order survive the best; the others are somewhat
like the rival cardinal cocks that Laurel and Miss Adele

watch fly and crash again and again into the bird-fright-
eners hanging in the fig trees. Their futile activity gets
them nowhere; they accomplish nothing.

Michael Kreyling and Ruth M. Vande Kieft have
both noted Miss Welty's extraordinary skill as a reader,
which in turn has made her an important reviewer and
essayist. Both have commented on the hallmark of her
criticism: it is a celebration of the art of writing, not mere
statements nor doctrines.[30] The spirit of celebration,
however, does not mean that Miss Welty refuses to chide;
she does, for example, in pointing out the infelicities
and unimaginative approach Arthur Mizener used in his
biography of Ford Madox Ford. Fifteen of her book reviews and twenty of her essays are included in *The Eye of
the Story* (1978), and to read one of her reviews carefully
is to be instructed in how to read judiciously and appre-
ciatively. Kreyling is quite correct in observing that by
reading and writing about other writers, Miss Welty has
shown readers how to read *her* work. In these essays and
reviews, Miss Welty defines, explains, and praises, often
in similes—a device not confined to her fiction. When
asked if she could talk about her use of metaphor (the
simile is the more frequent form in her writing), she
replied that she did not know how to, and explained why
by relating an anecdote about W. C. Fields. Having read
an analysis of how he juggled, Fields "couldn't juggle for
six years afterwards. He'd never known that was how it
was done. He'd just thrown up the balls and juggled."[31]
The similes are apt, and their sources are generally Miss
Welty's own observations or impressions of places, natural objects, and people. Only with examples can one
fully make a point. For instance, she describes Mizener's
prose juxtaposed with that of Ford's in this way: "To
read while they alternate is like being carried in a train
along the southern coast of France—long tunnel, view of
the sea, and over again." The 16,000-word sentence in
Faulkner's "The Bear" "races like a dinosaur across the

early fields of time." In her review of *The Underground Man*, Miss Welty praises Ross Macdonald's style saying it is "like a stand of clean, cool, well-branched, well-tended trees in which bright birds can flash and perch." Henry Green's novel *Living* "rushed forth like a pear tree into bloom on a black morning"; his short, glancing sentences produced an exhilarating effect "as when the knife thrower does not pierce but surrounds the living target, and it is the reader whose heart is thereby found." Even Green's repeating himself in *Nothing* and *Doting* was remarkable—"as if Daniel had got out of the lion's den twice in a row." Miss Welty's praise for Virginia Woolf had few limitations: "Hers was a sensitivity beside which a Geiger counter is a child's toy made of a couple of tin cans and a rather common piece of string. Allow it its blind spots, for it could detect pure gold." In commenting on the Nigel Nicolson and Joann Trautmann policy of including everything in Volume II of *The Letters of Virginia Woolf*, Miss Welty uses an extended simile of startling visual appeal: "The effect is one of profusion, like a spacious Edwardian flower bowl being constantly added to out of the advancing garden, useful little zinnias stuck in with the great peonies, spires of delphinium and the night stock, as they come into bloom." The six stories in Patrick White's *The Cockatoos* "go off like cannons fired over some popular scenic river—depth charges to bring up drowned bodies." In the autobiographical piece "A Sweet Devouring," Miss Welty writes: "The pleasures of reading itself—who doesn't remember?—were like those of a Christmas cake, a sweet devouring." She can juxtapose a homely image and a serious one. In her remarks before the American Academy of Arts and Letters and the National Institute of Arts and Letters upon the occasion of presenting the Gold Medal for Fiction to William Faulkner, Miss Welty said, "I think the medal, being pure of its kind, the real gold, would go to you of its own accord, and know its owner regardless of whether we were all here to see or not. *Safe as a puppy it would climb into your pocket* [italics added]."[32] Henry Green's novels "are provided with key settings and then the characters open their mouths and raise their novels from scratch" as if a housewife were making biscuits. Reading her essays and reviews discloses what Miss Welty feels about style, symbol, place, time, character, place names, the mystery of fiction, the reliability of a work of art. As a critic she provides insights into the work of others, into her own work, and into the whole craft of fiction.

In a 1965 essay, "Words into Fiction," Miss Welty discusses the elements of fiction writing and gives her most explicit statement about a writer's style, that element in the prose "which has constantly pressed to give the writing its objectivity." A highly conscious, but never a self-conscious, effort, style is something every serious writer has—"like the smoke from a fired cannon, like the ring in the water after the fish is pulled out or jumps back in." Style has to be found if the writing is to be done, but however good it is, Miss Welty "can't see that a writer deserves praise in particular for his style." More to be wished for is the reader's understanding of that style and the communication that follows. In the case of Henry Green's novels, the communication to Miss Welty as reader is quite distinct: "The spell comes each time from his style, a fact which explains nothing, for style is as mysterious a thing as any spell." Robert Penn Warren entitled his March 2, 1980, *New York Times Book Review* article "Under the Spell of Eudora Welty." Readers attest to the spell that comes each time through Miss Welty's style, but describing the parts is not to understand fully the mystery of the whole.

One distinctive aspect of her style is the use of detail, an aspect she commended in Willa Cather, who "saw her broad land in a sweep, but she saw selectively too—the detail that made all the difference." Washington Irving also comes in for praise: "Perhaps the most appealing thing about Irving here [*The Western Journals*] is his marvelous eye for detail—that dateless quality." Detail is a quality she admires also in Faulkner. When Carl Bundren "falls off the church roof he is perfectly well able to estimate the distance as 'twenty-eight foot, four and a half inches, about.' Faulkner had exactness."[33] Miss Welty's fund of details is wide, and her selection results in an object brought to life, a landscape graced with fruits and flowers, trees and birds, a character individualized. Told that one of the quilts Troy Flavin's mother sent as a wedding present (*Delta Wedding*) was called Delectable Mountains, a name also used in *Losing Battles*, Miss Welty did not recall the repetition, for she could have selected from the thirty quilt patterns that she knows. The Delectable Mountains pattern was chosen for its association with *Pilgrim's Progress*, and Granny's impending death is emphasized by Seek No Further, the burial quilt she has chosen. Troy Flavin, not distinguished for his cultural interests, proudly identified each quilt his mother sent—Dove in the Window, Tirzah's Treasures, Hearts and Gizzards, and Delectable Mountains. Katie Rainey's quilts (which Virgie says she will list in a For Sale ad once Katie is dead) include Double Muscadine Hulls, Road to Dublin, Starry Sky, Strange Spider Web, Hands All Around, and Double Wedding Ring. Always a visual writer, Miss Welty gives her readers a spate of colorful quilt names that tell stories of households where quilts were made, treasured, and handed down.

Details in Miss Welty's work are rarely insignificant because she strives to get everything right; she is a natural observer and to her "the detail tells everything. One detail can tell you more than any descriptive passage in general. . . . It goes back to place again. You've got to have everything truthful."[34] Miss Welty would have arrived at selecting the right details by herself, but some help came from an editor who told her long ago, "Don't ever have the moon in the wrong part of the sky," and from a reader of her early stories who wrote, "Dear Madame, I enjoyed your stories, but blue jays do not sit on railroad tracks." Sure enough, Miss Welty acknowledges, they do not.[35] The setting in many of the stories and novels is enriched with the flowers of Mississippi, and one feels Miss Welty knows all of them and their correct blooming season. Not merely do lilies grow, but in varieties called candlestick, water, milk-and-wine, blackberry, lemon, angel, and apostle; verbena comes in five colors; snow-on-the-mountain, four o'clocks, castor plants, angel trumpet, and night-blooming cereus appear. Aunt Ethel in "Kin" is a rose gardener and lovingly identifies each one—Souvenir de Claudius, Pernet, Mermaid, Mary Wallace, Silver Moon, Etoiles, Duquesa de Penaranda, Gruss an Aachen, Climbing Thorn. Clinton McKelva planted his favorite camellia on his wife's grave, the old-fashioned *Chandlerii Elegans* "now big as a pony, saddled with unplucked bloom living and dead, standing on a fading carpet of its own flowers." Fruit trees and berry briars are plentiful and tempting, the fig clearly the favorite and often of symbolic significance. Throughout Morgana, residents enjoy the pear, fig, and plum, the wild cherry, and the blackberry and elderberry patches. Other trees provide shade or ornamentation—crape-myrtle, mimosa, magnolia, sweet gum, sweet bay, cypress, swamp maple, live oak.

Although visual details are by far the most frequent, a catalog of odors in *Delta Wedding* makes the Fairchilds' store as real as any country store ever entered or imagined, each odor identifying a particular item and often calling forth a flood of memories.

All was warm and fragrant here. The cats smelled like ginger when you rubbed their blond foreheads and clasped their fat yellow sides. Every counter smelled different, from the ladylike smell of the dry-goods counter with its fussy revolving ball of string, to the manlike smell of coffee when it was ground in the back. There were areas of banana smell, medicine smell, rope and rubber and nail smell, bread smell, peppermint-oil smell, smells of feed, shot, cheese, tobacco, and chicory, and the smells of the old cane chairs creaking where the old fellows slept.

The details of a desk give well over a hundred years of its history. Becky McKelva had claimed for her use the plantation desk made of cherry trees from the McKelva place and bearing on the lid in different wood, 1817. It was graceful and small enough for a lady's desk; the double doors had no key, but Becky's privacy was itself inviolable. Family traits are revealed in a brief detail or two, as Miss Welty shows in *Losing Battles*. The Comfort family "never says 'Thank you' for a favor. They say that's because they're fully as good as you are." When Miss Lexie learns that Aycock Comfort is sitting in the Moodys' Buick, his weight keeping the car balanced on the precipice, she says, "Well, I'm gratified to hear it. I expect Parchman [the prison] did Aycock that much good. I wish you could find and send his daddy." When Aunt Cleo is told that Charlie Roy Hugg keeps the Ludlow jail, she wants to know how. "Drunk and two pistols. Makes his wife answer the phone." Aunt Nanny grins when she reports that "Stovalls fry their fish with the hides on," and when Aunt Cleo asks who *is* Willy Trimble, she gets an adequate characterization in one sentence. "'He's such a bachelor that the way he cleans out his fireplace is to carry the ashes through the house, shovel load at a time, and dump 'em through the front door!' said Miss Lexie Renfro. 'That answer your question?'"

Flannery O'Connor pointed out to Cecil Dawkins that in the manuscript version of her story "Hummers in the Larkspur" one of the women called her child "kid," a midwestern term heard only occasionally in the South. Miss O'Connor explained that "usually small-town Southerners if they aren't too common, call children children. Eudora Welty lets them say churren, which is

what they say. . . . I notice the poor white trashy kind in
the South call theirs 'younguns.'"[36] One word makes a
social and geographic distinction. Details perhaps are the
single most significant aspect of Miss Welty's style. No
matter how carefully chosen and used, a writer's sym-
bols, Miss Welty says, "are apt to be as swiftly spotted
by his reader as the smoke signals that once crossed our
plains from Indian to Indian. . . . How much brighter
than the symbol can be the explicit observation that
springs firsthand from deep and present feeling in one
breast." In writing dialogue she catches the sound and
cadence of each speaker and by his or her conversation
reveals and sometimes conceals parts of his or her personality. Subject matter, time, place, tone, and social
milieu differ radically, from the low middle-class gossip
in Leota's beauty parlor to the enigmatic thoughts and
conversations in "No Place for You, My Love," from the
internal monologue of the girl in "The Memory" to the
endless chatter of Losing Battles, from the boasting and
bickering in "The Wide Net" to the cryptic hints and inside jokes in "Powerhouse," from the small-town gossip
of The Ponder Heart to the poetic reflections in The Optimist's Daughter.

If any one word is characteristic of Eudora Welty,
the word is love, shorn of all sentimentality. When she
expresses her reaction to the work of her favorite authors—Jane Austen, Virginia Woolf, Elizabeth Bowen,
E. M. Forster, or Henry Green—it is to say that she
loves their work. She took her photographs in the 1930s
"because I loved them." Having read a portion of Losing
Battles on a public occasion, Miss Welty lowered the
book and said, "I love that part." If anyone has ever been
happy in a calling, it is Miss Welty. "I love to write. I'm
never happier than when I'm working. It doesn't matter
how hard it is; in fact, I love hard things to write. . . . I'm
utterly happy when I'm revising. Throwing away gives
me a great elation sometimes."[37] If one were counting,

Miss Welty used the word *love* at least twenty times in a recent television interview, and each time the word was apropos, genuine, unaffected. She herself might well be called an optimist's daughter, but one in whom the balance of sharp reality is never missing. The delight from her comedy never overshadows the total picture. After all, though Edna Earle Ponder continues to amuse readers, she is still a lonely spinster with hardly any hope that Mr. Springer will ever be anything more to her than just a guest at the Beulah Hotel. In praising E. B. White's *Charlotte's Web*, Miss Welty named qualities of fiction that, in turn, readers have continually praised in her work. "It has liveliness and felicity, tenderness and unexpectedness, grace and humor and praise of life, and the good backbone of succinctness that only the most highly imaginative stories possess."

If one were to choose a second word to characterize Miss Welty, a natural choice would be *integrity*, an indispensable quality of the true writer and one Miss Welty has said, "can be neither lost nor concealed nor faked nor quenched nor artificially come by nor outlived, nor, I believe, in the long run denied." In reviewing the *Selected Letters of William Faulkner*, Miss Welty ended by reminding the reader that Faulkner's fiction had been offered "to us from the start, and when we didn't even want it or know how to take it and understand it; it's been there all along and is more likely to remain. Read that." Miss Welty has been written about in pamphlets, articles, books, interviews, college term papers, theses, and dissertations and she will continue to be the subject of scholars' inquiry. The proliferation of critical studies is destined to continue, but Miss Welty's work is the most important thing and what the critic should say above all else is, "Read that."

Notes

1. WOMAN OF LETTERS: GREAT DESCENTS OF GOOD FORTUNE

1. Additional holdings are located at the University of Texas at Austin. All references to letters to and from Miss Welty and to other manuscript material are to the Eudora Welty Collection, Department of Archives and History, Jackson.

2. Linda Kuehl, "The Art of Fiction XLVII: Eudora Welty," *Paris Review*, XLVII (1972), 83–84.

3. Jane Reid Petty, "The town and the writer: An interview with Eudora Welty," *Jackson Magazine* (September 1977), p. 31.

4. Ibid., p. 35.

5. Eudora Welty, "A Salute from One of the Family," in *Lamar Life Insurance Company: A Tower of Strength in the Deep South, 50th Anniversary 1906–1956* (Montgomery: Paragon Press, [1956?]), p. 3. Subsequent references are to this text.

6. Jane Reid Petty, "The town and the writer: An interview with Eudora Welty," p. 30.

7. Matthew J. Bruccoli, *Conversations with Writers II* (Detroit: Gale Research Company, 1978), p. 292.

8. Victoria Glendinning, *Elizabeth Bowen* (New York: Avon Books, 1979), pp. 238–239.

9. "Images of the South: Visits with Eudora Welty and Walker Evans," *Southern Folklore Reports*, No. 1 (Memphis: Center for Southern Folklore, 1977), p. 21.

10. Charles T. Bunting, "'The Interior World': An Interview

with Eudora Welty," *Southern Review*, 8 (Autumn 1972), 726.

11. Robert Van Gelder, "An Interview with Eudora Welty," *Writers and Writing* (New York: Charles Scribner's Sons, 1946), p. 287.

12. Ruth M. Vande Kieft, *Eudora Welty* (New York: Twayne, 1962), p. 17.

13. Linda Kuehl, "The Art of Fiction XLVII: Eudora Welty," p. 88.

14. "Acrobats in a Park" was first published by M. Claude Richard in *Delta*, No. 5 (November 1977). Jan Nordby Gretlund published a revised version of the story in *South Carolina Review* 11, i (1978), 22–33; "The Doll" appeared in *The Tanager* (Grinnell College), 11 (June 1936), 11–14; "Magic" in *Manuscript*, 3 (September–October 1936), 3–7; and "Retreat" in *River*, I (March 1937), 10–12.

15. In time, Rood's artistic skills superseded his editorial interests, and the Contemporaries Gallery on Madison Avenue in New York City staged an Exhibition of Recent Sculpture by John Rood (Oct. 7–25, 1958). The handsome announcement contained a sketch by Miss Welty, who traced Rood's progress from "his early self-limiting reliance on wood alone" to his welding and constructing with glass and intractable metals. Miss Welty's praise was high, since she saw in Rood the true artist. "Maturity has simply assigned him to go ahead—the better he knows, the farther to try; the more he has to risk, to risk it. In the words of the highest praise any artist can give or receive, he goes out on a limb." In her customary lyric fashion, Miss Welty wrote that what John Rood had to say in his sculpture was "still fresh as a bird-call at morning."

16. Charlotte Capers, "The Narrow Escape of 'The [sic] Petrified Man': Early Eudora Welty Stories," *Journal of Mississippi History*, 41 (February 1979), 25–32.

17. Linda Kuehl, "The Art of Fiction XLVII: Eudora Welty," p. 90.

18. Charles Poore, "A Fine Novel of the Deep South," Review of *Delta Wedding*, in *New York Times Book Review* (14 April 1946), p. 1.

19. Linda Kuehl, "The Art of Fiction XLVII: Eudora Welty," p. 90.

20. Charles T. Bunting, "'The Interior World': An Interview with Eudora Welty," p. 713.

21. Subsequent references are to the typescript of *What Year Is This?* in the Eudora Welty Collection, Department of Archives and History, Jackson.

22. Jane Reid Petty, "The town and the writer: An interview with Eudora Welty," p. 34.

23. Ibid.

24. See Barbara McKenzie, "The Eye of Time: The Photographs of Eudora Welty," and Elizabeth Meese, "Constructing Time and Place: Eudora Welty in the Thirties," in *Eudora Welty: Critical Essays*, ed. Peggy W. Prenshaw (Jackson: University Press of Mississippi, 1979), pp. 386–400, 401–422; Guy Davenport, "Eudora Welty: Guy Davenport Celebrates a Writer and a Photographer," *Aperture*, No. 81 (1978), 48–59; and M. E. Bradford, "Miss Eudora's Picture Book," *Mississippi Quarterly*, 26, No. 4 (Fall 1973), 659–662. The September 1971 issue of *Mademoiselle* carried the introduction to *One Time, One Place*, along with several of the photographs.

2. THE PRISM OF COMEDY

1. Manuscript Letter, Eudora Welty Collection, Department of Archives and History, Jackson.

2. Linda Kuehl, "The Art of Fiction XLVII: Eudora Welty," *Paris Review*, XLVII (1972), 77.

3. Brom Weber, "The Mode of Black Humor," *The Comic Imagination in American Literature*, ed. Louis D. Rubin, Jr. (New Brunswick, N.J.: Rutgers University Press, 1973), p. 362.

4. The episode below occurred in Jamestown during the winter of 1609 and is presented in Walter Blair and Hamlin Hill, *America's Humor: From Poor Richard to Doonesbury* (New York: Oxford University Press, 1978), p. 7.

   One man murdered his wife, "powdered" [i.e. salted] her and, says Simmonds, "had eaten part of her before it was known: for which he was executed, as he well deserved. Now whether she was better roasted, boiled, or carbonado'd [broiled] I know not; but such a dish as powdered wife I never heard of."

5. Diana Trilling, Review of *Delta Wedding*, in *The Nation*, 162 (11 May 1946), 578.

6. Cleanth Brooks, "The Past Reexamined: *The Optimist's Daughter*," *Mississippi Quarterly*, 26 (Fall 1973), 578.

7. John F. Desmond, "Pattern and Vision in *The Optimist's Daughter*," *A Still Moment: Essays on the Art of Eudora Welty*, ed. John F. Desmond (Metuchen, N.J.: The Scarecrow Press, 1978), p. 122.

8. Cleanth Brooks, "Eudora Welty and the Southern Idiom," *Eudora Welty: A Form of Thanks*, ed. Louis Dollarhide and Ann J. Abadie (Jackson: University Press of Mississippi, 1979), p. 8.

9. Neil D. Isaacs, *Eudora Welty*, Southern Writers Series, No. 8 (Austin: Steck-Vaughn Company, 1969), p. 14. *The Ponder Heart* has enjoyed a considerable theatrical history. When Miss Welty was in Cambridge, England, in 1954, she wrote Danny Kaye hoping to interest him in a stage version. Although Kaye expressed admiration for Miss Welty's work, previous commitments kept him from undertaking the role of Uncle Daniel. Although the Chodorov and Fields adaptation was successful, they deserted Edna Earle as the established point of view; as a result, Miss Welty found the texture of the play thin. Characters' idiosyncrasies just exist, she contended, they cannot be explained by realistic cause and effect. Miss Welty's annotations on the script indicate that Chodorov and Fields did not get enough local color on their trip to Jackson. For example, they had a mourning band on Uncle Daniel's arm, something "nobody does in little towns"; Mrs. Peacock would say "dinner," not "lunch"; the cry into the telephone would not be "Operator! Operator!" but "Central! Central!" For further discussion of the novel and play differences, see Brenda G. Cornell, "Ambiguous Necessity: A Study of *The Ponder Heart*," *Eudora Welty: Critical Essays*, ed. Peggy W. Prenshaw (Jackson: University Press of Mississippi, 1979), pp. 208–219.

10. Ruth M. Vande Kieft, "Looking with Eudora Welty," *Eudora Welty: Critical Essays*, ed. Peggy W. Prenshaw (Jackson: University Press of Mississippi, 1979), p. 441.

11. Seymour Gross, "A Long Day's Living: The Angelic In-

genuities of *Losing Battles*," *Eudora Welty: Critical Essays*, ed. Peggy W. Prenshaw (Jackson: University Press of Mississippi, 1979), p. 340.

12. Charles T. Bunting, "'The Interior World': An Interview with Eudora Welty," *Southern Review*, 8 (Autumn 1972), 726.

13. Walter Blair and Hamlin Hill, *American Humor: From Poor Richard to Doonesbury* (New York: Oxford University Press, 1978), p. 466.

3.   DELIGHT ENDING IN WISDOM

1. Eudora Welty, *Selected Stories of Eudora Welty* with an introduction by Katherine Anne Porter (New York: Modern Library, 1954), pp. xiii, xix.

2. Jean Stafford, Review of *The Wide Net*, in *Partisan Review*, 11 (Winter 1944), 114. (Includes remarks on *A Curtain of Green*.)

3. Marianne Hauser, Review of *A Curtain of Green*, in *New York Times Book Review* (16 November 1941), p. 6.

4. Ruth M. Vande Kieft, Review of Victor H. Thompson, *Eudora Welty: A Reference Guide*, in *Mississippi Quarterly*, 30 (Winter 1976–77), 75.

5. Elizabeth Bowen, Review of *The Golden Apples*, in *Seven Winters and Afterthoughts* (New York: Knopf, 1962), pp. 215–216.

6. Jane Reid Petty, "The town and the writer: An interview with Eudora Welty," *Jackson Magazine* (September 1977), pp. 34–35.

7. Robert B. Heilman, "Salesman's Deaths: Documentary and Myth," *Shenandoah*, 20 (Spring 1969), 20–28.

8. Linda Kuehl, "The Art of Fiction XLVII: Eudora Welty," *Paris Review*, XLVII (1972), 81.

9. Elizabeth Bowen, *Afterthoughts: Pieces about Writing* (London: Longmans, 1962), p. 173.

10. ———, "Enchanted Centenary of the Brothers Grimm," *New York Times Book Review* (8 September 1963), p. 113.

11. Michael Kreyling, "Clement and the Indians: Pastoral and History in *The Robber Bridegroom*," *Eudora Welty: A*

Form of Thanks, ed. Louis Dollarhide and Ann J. Abadie (Jackson: University Press of Mississippi, 1979), p. 27.

12. ————, *Eudora Welty* (Jackson: Mississippi Library Commission, 1976), n.p.

13. Alfred Kazin, Review of *The Robber Bridegroom*, in *New York Herald Tribune* (25 October 1942), p. 19.

14. Charles T. Bunting, "'The Interior World': An Interview with Eudora Welty," *Southern Review*, 8 (Autumn 1972), p. 714.

15. Thomas L. McHaney, "Eudora Welty and the Multitudinous Golden Apples," *Mississippi Quarterly*, 26 (Fall 1973), 590.

16. William F. Buckley, "The Southern Imagination: An Interview with Eudora Welty and Walker Percy," *Mississippi Quarterly*, 26 (Fall 1973), 510.

17. Linda Kuehl, "The Art of Fiction XLVII: Eudora Welty," 93.

18. Typescript of *The Golden Apples*, Eudora Welty Collection, Department of Archives and History, Jackson.

19. Philip L. Miller, *The Ring of Words: An Anthology of Song Texts* (New York: W. W. Norton, 1963), pp. xxiii–ix.

20. Ruth M. Vande Kieft, *Eudora Welty* (New York: Twayne, 1962), p. 142.

21. Merrill M. Skaggs, "Morgana's Apples and Pears," *Eudora Welty: Critical Essays*, ed. Peggy W. Prenshaw (Jackson: University Press of Mississippi, 1979), p. 241.

22. Robert Heilman, "*Losing Battles* and Winning the War," *Eudora Welty: Critical Essays*, ed. Peggy W. Prenshaw (Jackson: University Press of Mississippi, 1979), pp. 303–304.

23. James Boatwright, "Speech and Silence in *Losing Battles*," *Shenandoah*, 25 (Spring 1974), 5.

24. Ibid., p. 12.

25. Linda Kuehl, "The Art of Fiction XLVII: Eudora Welty," p. 85.

26. Charles T. Bunting, "'The Interior World': An Interview with Eudora Welty," p. 720.

27. Ruth M. Vande Kieft, "The Vision of Eudora Welty," *Mississippi Quarterly*, 26 (Fall 1973), 535.

28. Robert Heilman, "*Losing Battles* and Winning the War," p. 274.

29. Mary Anne Ferguson, "*Losing Battles* as a Comic Epic in Prose," *Eudora Welty: Critical Essays*, ed. Peggy W. Prenshaw (Jackson: University Press of Mississippi, 1979), p. 308.

30. Ibid., p. 309.

31. Seymour Gross, "A Long Day's Living: The Angelic Ingenuities of *Losing Battles*," *Eudora Welty: Critical Essays*, ed. Peggy W. Prenshaw (Jackson: University Press of Mississippi, 1979), p. 336.

32. Louis D. Rubin, Jr., "Everything Brought Out in the Open: Eudora Welty's *Losing Battles*," *Hollins Critic*, 7 (June 1970), 2.

33. Elmo Howell, "Eudora Welty and the City of Man," *Georgia Review*, 33 (Winter 1979), 771.

34. Louis D. Rubin, Jr., "Everything Brought Out in the Open: Eudora Welty's *Losing Battles*," p. 12.

4. VORTEXES OF QUIET

1. Jean Stafford, Review of *The Wide Net*, in *Partisan Review*, 11 (Winter 1944), 115.

2. Leo Lerman, Review of *The Wide Net*, in *New York Herald Tribune Book Review* (26 September 1943), p. 4.

3. Robert Penn Warren, "The Love and the Separateness in Miss Welty's Fiction," *Kenyon Review*, 6 (1944), 246–259.

4. Albert J. Devlin, "Eudora Welty's Historicism: Method and Vision," *Mississippi Quarterly*, 30 (1976–77), 214.

5. Charles T. Bunting, "'The Interior World': An Interview with Eudora Welty," *Southern Review*, 8 (Autumn 1972), 735.

6. Neil D. Isaacs, *Eudora Welty* (Austin: Steck-Vaughn, 1969), p. 19.

7. Anne M. Messerand, "Eudora Welty's Travellers: The Journey Theme in Her Short Stories," *Southern Literary Journal*, 3 (1971), 45.

8. Joyce Carol Oates, "The Art of Eudora Welty," *Shenandoah*, 20 (1969), 54.

9. J. A. Bryant, Jr., *Eudora Welty* (Minneapolis: University of Minnesota Press, 1968), p. 24.

10. Charles T. Bunting, "'The Interior World': An Interview

with Eudora Welty," p. 721. One of the best and most recent treatments of *Delta Wedding* is Michael Kreyling's chapter, "Finding a Style: 'The Delta Cousins' into *Delta Wedding*" in his *Eudora Welty's Achievement of Order* (Baton Rouge: Louisiana State University Press, 1980) pp. 52–76. Kreyling traces the changes in style that the unpublished story "The Delta Cousins" (a work Miss Welty's agent Diarmuid Russell returned with the message, this is chapter two of a novel) underwent in becoming *Delta Wedding*. Some characters' names changed (Aunt Min to Ellen, Raymond to George), the Sunflower River became the Yazoo (River of Death), the important confrontation of India and Laura with the bee man was significantly altered. The vital change, Kreyling quite rightly notes, "is the technical choice that shifts the novel from narrative to lyric; it presents the characters as stanzas in a poem about love, need, and sympathy" (p. 61).

11. M. E. Bradford, "Fairchild as Composite Protagonist," *Eudora Welty: Critical Essays*, ed. Peggy W. Prenshaw (Jackson: University Press of Mississippi, 1979), p. 202.

12. John Alexander Allen, "The Other Way To Live: Demigods in Eudora Welty's Fiction," *Eudora Welty: Critical Essays*, ed. Peggy W. Prenshaw (Jackson: University Press of Mississippi, 1979), p. 38.

13. Ruth M. Vande Kieft, *Eudora Welty* (New York: Twayne, 1962), p. 152.

14. Noel Polk, "Water, Wanderers, and Weddings: Love in Eudora Welty," *Eudora Welty: A Form of Thanks*, ed. Louis Dollarhide and Ann J. Abadie (Jackson: University Press of Mississippi, 1979), p. 116.

15. Orville Prescott, Review of *The Bride of Innisfallen*, in *New York Times* (8 April 1955), p. 19.

16. Cleanth Brooks, "The Past Reexamined: *The Optimist's Daughter*," *Mississippi Quarterly*, 27 (Fall 1973), 582.

17. John F. Desmond, "Pattern and Vision in *The Optimist's Daughter*," *A Still Moment: Essays on the Art of Eudora Welty*, ed. John F. Desmond (Metuchen, N.J.: Scarecrow Press, 1978), p. 133.

18. Cleanth Brooks, "The Past Reexamined: *The Optimist's Daughter*," p. 577.

5. THE HIGH ART OF EUDORA WELTY

1. Orville Prescott, "A Handful of Rising Stars," *New York Times Book Review* (21 March 1943), p. 13.

2. Linda Kuehl, "The Art of Fiction XLVII: Eudora Welty," *Paris Review*, XLVII (1972), 95.

3. Eudora Welty, "Looking Back at the First Story," *Georgia Review*, 33 (Winter 1979), 751–752.

4. Louis D. Rubin, Jr., *William Elliott Shoots a Bear: Essays on the Southern Literary Imagination* (Baton Rouge: Louisiana State University Press, 1975), p. 200.

5. C. Hugh Holman, *The Roots of Southern Writing: Essays on the Literature of the American South* (Athens: University of Georgia Press, 1972), pp. 89–90.

6. In "Place in Fiction," Miss Welty asks, "Might the magic lie partly, too, in the *name* of the place—since that is what *we* gave it?"

7. Eudora Welty, "Looking Back at the First Story," p. 754. In a 1972 interview, Miss Welty commented on her selection of characters' names. "But I wouldn't ever use a name that was right in feeling if it weren't also typical of the kind of people. I'm careful as I can be about names, and I work hard at them." Charles T. Bunting, "'The Interior World': An Interview with Eudora Welty," *Southern Review*, 8 (Autumn 1972), 723.

8. Frederick J. Hoffman, *The Art of Southern Fiction* (Carbondale: Southern Illinois University Press, 1967), pp. 4, 11.

9. Ibid., p. 23.

10. Ibid., p. 27.

11. Linda Kuehl, "The Art of Fiction XLVII: Eudora Welty," p. 91.

12. Robert Penn Warren, "Under the Spell of Eudora Welty," *New York Times Book Review* (2 March 1980), p. 1.

13. William F. Buckley, "The Southern Imagination: An Interview with Eudora Welty and Walker Percy," *Mississippi Quarterly*, 26 (1973), 499.

14. Linda Kuehl, "The Art of Fiction XLVII: Eudora Welty," p. 80.

15. "Images of the South: Visits with Eudora Welty and Walker Evans," *Southern Folklore Reports*, No. 1 (Memphis: Center for Southern Folklore, 1977), p. 21.

16. J. A. Bryant, Jr., *Eudora Welty* (Minneapolis: University of Minnesota Press, 1968), p. 20.

17. Margaret Marshall, "Notes by the Way," *The Nation*, 169 (10 September 1949), 256.

18. Walter Sullivan, *A Requiem for the Renascence: The State of Fiction in the Modern South* (Athens: University of Georgia Press, 1976), p. xxi.

19. "Images of the South: Visits with Eudora Welty and Walker Evans," p. 23.

20. Seymour Gross and John E. Hardy, *Images of the Negro in American Literature* (Chicago: University of Illinois Press, 1966), p. 221.

21. Alfred Appel, Jr., *A Season of Dreams: The Fiction of Eudora Welty* (Baton Rouge: Louisiana State University Press, 1965), p. 146.

22. Seymour Gross and John E. Hardy, *Images of the Negro in American Literature*, p. 229.

23. An early version using this title appeared in *Write and Rewrite: A Study of the Creative Process*, ed. John Kuehl (New York: Meredith Press, 1967), pp. 4–14.

24. Linda Kuehl, "The Art of Fiction XLVII: Eudora Welty," p. 87.

25. *The Letters of Flannery O'Connor: The Habit of Being*, ed. Sally Fitzgerald (New York: Farrar, Straus and Giroux, 1979), p. 533.

26. Ibid., p. 537.

27. Charles T. Bunting, "'The Interior World': An Interview with Eudora Welty," *Southern Review*, 8 (Autumn 1972) 724.

28. Linda Kuehl, "The Art of Fiction XLVII: Eudora Welty," pp. 95–96.

29. Michael Kreyling, *Eudora Welty's Achievement of Order* (Baton Rouge: Louisiana State University Press, 1980), p. 156.

30. Michael Kreyling, "Words into Criticism: Eudora Welty's Essays and Reviews," and Ruth M. Vande Kieft, "Looking with Eudora Welty," *Eudora Welty: Critical Essays*,

ed. Peggy W. Prenshaw (Jackson: University Press of Mississippi, 1979), pp. 411–422; 423–444.

31. Linda Kuehl, "The Art of Fiction XLVII: Eudora Welty," p. 97.

32. Eudora Welty, "Presentation to William Faulkner of the Gold Medal for Fiction," *Proceedings of the American Academy of Arts and Letters and the National Institute of Arts and Letters*, Second Series, No. 13 (New York, 1963), p. 225.

33. Southern Literary Festival Speech (Oxford, Miss., 23 April 1965).

34. "Images of the South: Visits with Eudora Welty and Walker Evans," p. 20.

35. Ibid., pp. 19–20.

36. *The Letters of Flannery O'Connor*, ed. Sally Fitzgerald, p. 296.

37. Charles T. Bunting, "'The Interior World': An Interview with Eudora Welty," p. 732.

Bibliography

WORKS BY EUDORA WELTY

Fiction

A Curtain of Green and Other Stories, with an introduction by Katherine Anne Porter. Garden City, N.Y.: Doubleday Doran, 1941.

The Robber Bridegroom. Garden City, N.Y.: Doubleday Doran, 1942.

The Wide Net and Other Stories. New York: Harcourt Brace, 1943.

Delta Wedding. New York: Harcourt Brace, 1946.

Music from Spain. Greenville, Miss.: Levee Press, 1948.

The Golden Apples. New York: Harcourt Brace, 1949.

The Ponder Heart. New York: Harcourt Brace, 1954.

Selected Stories. New York: Modern Library, 1954.

The Bride of Innisfallen. New York: Harcourt Brace, 1955.

The Shoe Bird. New York: Harcourt Brace, 1964.

Thirteen Stories, with an introduction by Ruth M. Vande Kieft. New York: Harcourt Brace, 1965.

Losing Battles. New York: Random House, 1970.

The Optimist's Daughter. New York: Random House, 1972.

The Collected Stories of Eudora Welty. New York: Harcourt Brace Jovanovich, 1980.

Uncollected Stories

"The Doll," *The Tanager* (Grinnell College, Grinnell, Iowa), 11 (June 1936), 11–14.

"Magic," *Manuscript*, 3 (September–October 1936), 3–7.

"Retreat," *River*, 1 (March 1937), 10–12.

"A Sketching Trip," *Atlantic Monthly*, 175 (June 1945), 62–70.

"Hello and Good-Bye," *Atlantic Monthly*, 180 (July 1947), 37–40.

"Acrobats in a Park," *South Carolina Review*, 11 (1978), 26–33.

Nonfiction

The Reading and Writing of Short Stories. Atlantic, 183 (February 1949), 54–58.

Place in Fiction. New York: House of Books, 1957.

Three Papers on Fiction. New York: Harcourt Brace, 1957.

A Sweet Devouring. New York: Albondocani Press, 1969.

One Time, One Place: Mississippi in the Depression: A Snapshot Album, with introduction by Eudora Welty. New York: Random House, 1971.

A Pageant of Birds. New York: Albondocani Press, 1974.

Fairy Tale of the Natchez Trace. Jackson: Mississippi Historical Society, 1975.

The Eye of the Story: Selected Essays and Reviews. New York: Random House, 1978.

Ida M'Toy. Urbana: University of Illinois Press, 1979.

Eudora Welty: Twenty Photographs. Winston-Salem, N.C.: Palaemon Press, 1980.

Uncollected Essays. (See Noel Polk bibliography and the *Eudora Welty Newsletter* for citations of book reviews.)

Women!! Make Turban in Own Home! *Junior League Magazine*, 28 (November 1941), 20–21, 62.

"Jose De Creeft," *Magazine of Art*, 37 (February 1944), 42–47.

"Literature and the Lens," *Vogue*, 104 (1 August 1944), 102–103.

"Department of Amplification" (Letter Protesting Edmund Wilson's review of William Faulkner's *Intruder in the Dust*), *New Yorker*, 24 (1 January 1959), 50–51.

"Good Intentions," *New York Times Book Review* (31 December 1950), p. 8.

"The Concept in Review," *Concept* (Converse College), 50 (May 1951), 4, 12.

"The Abode of Summer," *Harper's Bazaar* (June 1952), 50, 115.

"Is There a Reader in the House?" *Mississippi Educational Advance*, 47 (November 1955), 12–13.

"The Right to Read," *Mississippi Magic*, 16 (May 1961), 15.

"Author Gave Life to Fictional County," *Washington Post and Times-Herald* (7 July 1962), p. 2-C.

"And They All Lived Happily Ever After," *New York Times Book Review*, Part II (10 November 1963), p. 3.

"Tribute to Flannery O'Connor," *Esprit* (University of Scranton), 8 (Winter 1964), 49.

"English from the Inside," *American Education*, 2 (February 1966), 18–19.

"From Where I Live," *Delta Review*, 6 (November–December 1969), 69.

"Looking Back at the First Story," *Georgia Review*, 33 (Winter 1979, 751–769.

WORKS ABOUT EUDORA WELTY

Bibliographies

Bibliographies of Eudora Welty's work first appeared in 1956. In addition to the titles below, the reader should also consult *The Eudora Welty Newsletter* for checklists of Welty scholarship since 1975.

Cole, McKelva. "Book Reviews by Eudora Welty: A Checklist," *Bulletin of Bibliography*, 23 (January–April 1963), 240.

Gross, Seymour L. "Eudora Welty: A Bibliography of Criticism and Comment," Secretary's News Sheet, Bibliography Society, University of Virginia, No. 45 (April 1960).

Jordan, Leona. "Eudora Welty: Selected Criticism," *Bulletin of Bibliography*, 23 (January–April 1960), 14–15.

McDonald, W. U., Jr. "Eudora Welty Manuscripts: An Annotated Finding List," *Bulletin of Bibliography*, 24 (September–December 1963), 44–46.

Polk, Noel. "A Eudora Welty Checklist," *Mississippi Quarterly*, 26 (Fall 1973), 663–693.

Thompson, Victor H. *Eudora Welty: A Reference Guide*. Boston: G. K. Hall, 1976.

Books, Pamphlets, Special Issues of Journals

Appel, Alfred, Jr. *A Season of Dreams: The Fiction of Eudora Welty*. Baton Rouge: Louisiana State University Press, 1965.

Boatwright, James (ed.). *Special Issue: A Tribute to Eudora Welty. Shenandoah, The Washington and Lee Review*, Vol. 20, No. 3 (Spring 1969).

Bryant, J. A., Jr. *Eudora Welty* (Minnesota Pamphlet No. 66). Minneapolis: University of Minnesota Press, 1968.

Desmond, John F. (ed.). *A Still Moment: Essays on the Art of Eudora Welty*. Metuchen, N.J.: Scarecrow Press, 1978.

Dollarhide, Louis and Abadie, Ann J. (eds.). *Eudora Welty: A Form of Thanks*. Jackson: University Press of Mississippi, 1979.

Howard, Zelma Turner. *The Rhetoric of Eudora Welty's Short Stories*. Jackson: University and College Press of Mississippi Monograph Series—Humanities, 1973.

Isaacs, Neil D. *Eudora Welty* (Steck-Vaughn Southern Writers Series, No. 8). Austin, Texas: Steck-Vaughn, 1969.

Kreyling, Michael. *Eudora Welty's Achievement of Order*. Baton Rouge: Louisiana State University Press, 1980.

Manz-Kunz, Marie-Antoinette. *Eudora Welty: Aspects of Reality in Her Short Fiction*. Bern, Switzerland: Francke Verlag, 1971.

Prenshaw, Peggy W. (ed.). *Eudora Welty: Critical Essays*. Jackson: University Press of Mississippi, 1979.

Eudora Welty Issue, Delta Review, No. 5 (November 1977).

Vande Kieft, Ruth M. *Eudora Welty*. New York: Twayne, 1962.

Williams, Peyton, Jr. (ed.). *Special Issue: Eudora Welty, Mississippi Quarterly*, Vol. 26 (Fall 1973).

Selected Articles

Daniel, Robert. "The World of Eudora Welty," *Hopkins Review*, 6 (Winter 1953), 49–58.

Howell, Elmo. "Eudora Welty and the City of Man," *Georgia Review*, 33 (Winter 1979), 770–782.

————. "Eudora Welty and the Use of Place in Southern Fiction," *Arizona Quarterly*, 28 (Autumn 1972), 248–256.

Glenn, Eunice. "Fantasy in the Fiction of Eudora Welty," in *A Southern Vanguard*, ed. Allen Tate. New York: Prentice Hall, 1947, pp. 117–124.

Gossett, Louise Y. "Violence as Revelation: Eudora Welty,"

in *Violence in Recent Southern Fiction*. Durham: Duke University Press, 1965, pp. 98–117.

MacKethan, Lucinda H. "To See Things in Their Time: The Art of Focus in Eudora Welty's Fiction," *American Literature*, 10 (1978), 258–275.

Masserand, Anne M. "Eudora Welty's Travellers: The Journey Theme in Her Short Stories," *Southern Literary Journal*, 3 (1971), 39–48.

Messerli, Douglas. "The Problem of Time in Welty's *Delta Wedding*," *Studies in American Fiction*, 5 (1977–78), 227–240.

Rubin, Louis D., Jr. "Everything Brought Out into the Open: Eudora Welty's *Losing Battles*," in *William Elliott Shoots a Bear: Essays on the Southern Literary Imagination*. Baton Rouge: Louisiana State University Press, 1975, pp. 213–225.

Slethang, Gordon E. "Initiation in Eudora Welty's *The Robber Bridegroom*," *Southern Humanities Review*, 7 (Winter 1973), 77–87.

Stuckey, William J. "The Use of Marriage in Welty's *The Optimist's Daughter*," *Critique*, 17 (1975), 36–46.

Warren, Robert Penn. "The Love and the Separateness in Miss Welty," *Kenyon Review*, 6 (Spring 1944), 246–259.

Selected Interviews

Bruccoli, Matthew J. *Eudora Welty*, in *Conversations with Writers II*. Detroit: Gale Research Company, 1978, pp. 285–316.

Buckley, William F., Jr. "The Southern Imagination": Interview with Eudora Welty and Walker Percy, on Firing Line, television broadcast of 24 December 1972. Reprinted in *Mississippi Quarterly*, 26 (Fall 1973), 493–516.

Bunting, Charles T. "'The Interior World': An Interview with Eudora Welty," *Southern Review*, 8 (October 1972), 711–735.

"Images of the South: Visits with Eudora Welty and Walker Evans," *Southern Folklore Reports*, No. 1. Memphis: Center for Southern Folklore, 1977, pp. 12–26.

Kuehl, Linda. "The Art of Fiction XLVII: Eudora Welty," *Paris Review*, XLVII, 55 (Fall 1972), pp. 72–97.

Nostrandt, Jeanne Rolfe. "Fiction as Event: An Interview with

Eudora Welty," *New Orleans Review*, 7, No. 1 (1979), 26–34.

Petty, Jane Reid. "The town and the writer: An interview with Eudora Welty," *Jackson Magazine* (September 1977), 29–35.

Van Gelder, Robert. "An Interview with Eudora Welty," *Writers and Writing*. New York: Scribner's, 1946, pp. 287–290.

Walker, Alice. "Eudora Welty: An Interview," *Harvard Advocate*, 106 (Winter 1973), 68–72.

Index

MODERN LITERATURE SERIES

In the same series (continued from page ii)